The
SISTER BLOCKS

17 sisterly sets from The Kansas City Star

Redrafts, instruction, templates ✄ plus seven new Star patterns

Edie McGinnis

KANSAS CITY STAR BOOKS

Preceding page: Sampler quilt made in the '30s by Mrs. R. E. De Lancy from patterns printed in
The Kansas City Star. The quilt is owned by her granddaughter, Gayle Buckley Carlton.

Left: Edie McGinnis (left) and her sister Stormy Lee.

The Sister Blocks
Author: Edie McGinnis

Editor: Doug Weaver
Design: River City Studio, Kansas City, Mo.

Illustrations: Gary Embrey
Photography: Susan Pfannmuller
Published by
KANSAS CITY STAR BOOKS
1729 Grand Blvd.
Kansas City, Missouri, USA 64108

First edition

Library of Congress Card Number:
2001093200

ISBN 0-9709131-9-2

Printed in the United States of America
by Jostens, Topeka, Kan.

To order copies, call StarInfo at
(816) 234-4636 and say "Books."
Or go to www.PickleDish.com.

Any pattern designs bearing a resemblance
to original designs in this book are
purely unintentional.

Acknowledgements

Many thanks go to the ladies who made the blocks and tested out the patterns. This book wouldn't exist without them — Sharon McMillan (my big sister), Marquette Heights, Ill.; Peggy McFeeters, Morton, Ill.; Sue McNamara and Debbie Pulley, Peoria, Ill.; Cecelia Ash and Barbara Maxwell of Pekin, Ill.; Nancy Dietz, Lenexa, Ks.; Ruth Lofgren, Fort Leavenworth, Ks. My friends from Calico Cutups; Florence Bessmer, Buckner, Mo.; Ruby Downing, Oak Grove, Mo.; Betty Stubler, Smithville, Mo.; Jennie Crawford, Liberty, Mo.; Arlene Johnson, Kansas City, Mo.; Corky and Peggy Hutinett of Raytown, Mo.; and Clara Diaz, Helen Johnson, Rosemary Garten, Donna English, Alta Short, Mary Ellen Bloomquist, Vera Doutt, Millie Hohimer, Linda Kriesel and Judy Lovell, all of Independence, Mo.

Thanks to Judy Streu of Liberty, Mo., for sharing her wonderful quilts, her time and her ladders with us.

Thanks to Morgan and Jessica Elliot and Courtney Fiser for their patience with the photographer.

I appreciate all the responses to our quest for quilts to photograph for this book. Some people came from quite a distance and I thank them for letting us enjoy their quilts.

Thanks also to Susan Pfannmuller, our photographer, and the folks at River City Studio for their artwork, and Doug Weaver, the editor of this book who now knows more about quilting than he ever wanted to or thought possible.

Bibliography
References: 1. The Tennessean Travel Section. "Warm Springs: A Turning Point For The World," by Linda Quigley. 2. 1997 Paralyzed Veterans of America Paraplegia News, "A Warm Welcome at Warm Springs: Roosevelt Warm Springs Institute for Rehabilitation" by Cliff Crase. 3. *The Kansas City Star*, 1/27/34.

Table *of* Contents

Introduction

Shari McMillan

Stormy van den Houghten

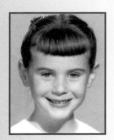

Barb Owen

Jane Hoover

I n my years of quilting I have made a remarkable and wondrous discovery. I have found an extended family far beyond my wildest dreams. I have shopped far and wide for fabric and have written checks to shop owners who don't know me, in towns I have not been in before and will probably never be in again. When I asked if these people wanted my driver's license number and identification, I was generally told no because they had never received a bad check from a quilter.

I have been a member of more than one quilt guild and I have needed help with a quilt or a pattern many times. I have found that if I travel to my nearest quilt shop or call my quilting friends, I will have all the help a person could ever ask for.

I have seen guild members make quilts for friends, relatives, people in need, children with AIDS, children who needed comfort, for the police force to carry in their squad cars to hand out as they saw fit, for children in battered women's shelters and to benefit all sorts of organizations and charities. I have seen people who would not consider selling a quilt give one away in a heartbeat. I have seen a fabric stash replenished by donations when a fellow quilter had lost hers in a fire. Fabric and patterns are traded and books are lent to one another as a matter of course in this sisterhood to which I am honored to belong.

I have two sisters, Shari and Stormy Lee, who arrived in our family before I did. We were raised in a different era then. We had to help out and be responsible at an early age because my mother worked. I've often felt badly as an adult for my oldest sister, because she got stuck with the job of taking care of my sister and me. It's a good thing we were such angels! (Yeah, right!) We did survive our childhood without killing one another and have gotten to be pretty decent friends. We also have quite a few things in common. We all had children — boys. We all like to read. We all make lovely things.

Shari makes quilts, bobbin lace, Hardanger lace and she tats and crochets and knits. Stormy makes bobbin lace and has won ribbons in fairs and sells her work. I crochet and make quilts and

> **❝** This book and these blocks are for the sisters we all share, related by blood or by friendship or by choice. It makes no difference, because the quilting is in our hearts and is there to be shared. **❞**

am learning to tat. We all giggle with one another over the phone and share a very wry sense of humor.

I am very proud of my sisters and I love them to pieces. The one thing that makes me sad is the fact that we live so far apart. Of course, sometimes I guess that is a good thing, especially when we have a difference of opinion or manage to irritate one another. But most of the time, I just miss them and wish I could take a quilt I am working on over to their house and sit and drink coffee and chat without driving for seven hours or flying to the West Coast.

Since we live so far apart I have been very fortunate to have gathered a different set of sisters. They are sisters of my heart. Jane, Nancy, Norma, Barb and Peg are the kind of friends one would choose to be their sisters. We are all pretty much alike when it comes to what we cherish in other people. None of us suffers fools gladly, we all like to laugh a lot and we all feel obligated to keep each other's secrets. We can be as silly as we like without feeling self-conscious and we can have those serious heart-to-heart talks. We lift each other up and listen with our hearts. I don't believe there is anything we would not do for each other if it were possible.

This book and these blocks are for the sisters we all share, related by blood or by friendship or by choice. It makes no difference, because the quilting is in our hearts and is there to be shared.

The following pages contain sets of sister blocks. For each pieced block there is an applique block. The blocks generally share a common name. Sometimes they look a great deal alike, sometimes they don't. All but seven of them are from the collection of *The Kansas City Star*. The others are original designs of my own.

Enjoy.

Edie McGinnis

Nancy Caldwell

Norma Phillips

Peggy Hutinett

Edie McGinnis

… has been quilting for about 25 years. She was a member of Boonslick Trail Quilting Guild in Columbia, Mo. She is presently a member of the American Quilter's Society and the Calico Cut-ups Quilting Club of Independence, Mo. This is the fourth quilt book Edie has been involved with pertaining to the Kansas City Star Quilt patterns.

Photo of Edie McGinnis by Steve Gonzales of The Kansas City Star.

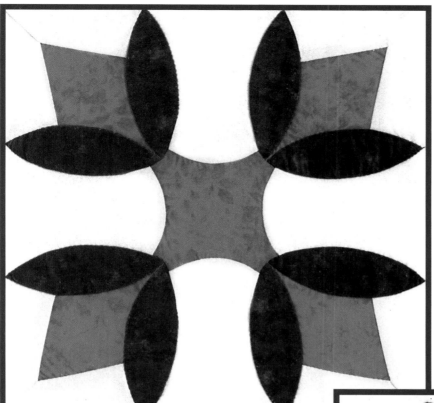

A Century Old Tulip block pieced by Florence Bessmer of Buckner, Mo.

Dutch Tulip block appliqued by Jennie Crawford of Liberty, Mo.

THE
Tulips

My sisters and I grew up in Tremont, Ill. When I went to the house of one of my friends, I had to walk past a big, old Victorian house that sat a long way back from the edge of the street. I don't remember the name of the old man that lived there, but I do remember being afraid of him.

In the ditch in front of the yard and sidewalk, a profusion of tulips and daffodils bloomed every spring. One year I convinced myself that since the flowers were growing in the ditch there would be no harm in picking a big bouquet of them. I was also sure that since the house was so far away from the street no one would see me anyway. I sat down and had gathered quite a large handful of flowers when I had the eerie feeling that there was someone behind me.

Sure enough, that old man was standing there. Before he could say a word, I handed the flowers to him and said, "Here mister, I was just getting ready to bring these to you so you could have a bouquet for your table."

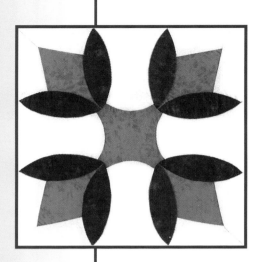

A Century Old Tulip Pattern

September 24, 1947
12" Block

Fabric needed: White, green and red.

From the white fabric, cut 4 pieces using template B, 4 pieces using template A and 4 pieces using template C.

From green fabric, cut 8 pieces using template D.

From red fabric, cut 4 pieces using template E and one piece using template F.

Sew a white C piece to a red E piece.

Add the white A piece next.

Now sew a green oval to each side.

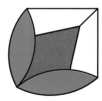

Make three more of these corner units.

Sew a white B piece to each side of the red F piece.

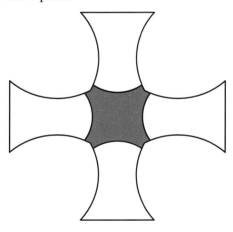

Set in each corner unit to complete the block.

A Century Old Tulip

TEMPLATE

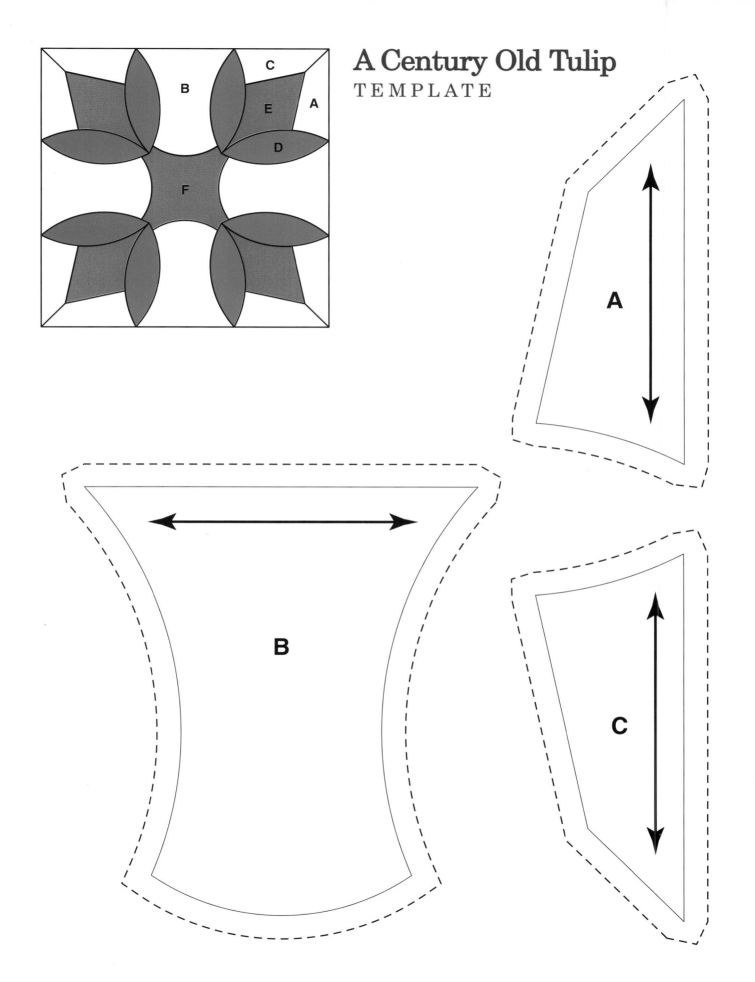

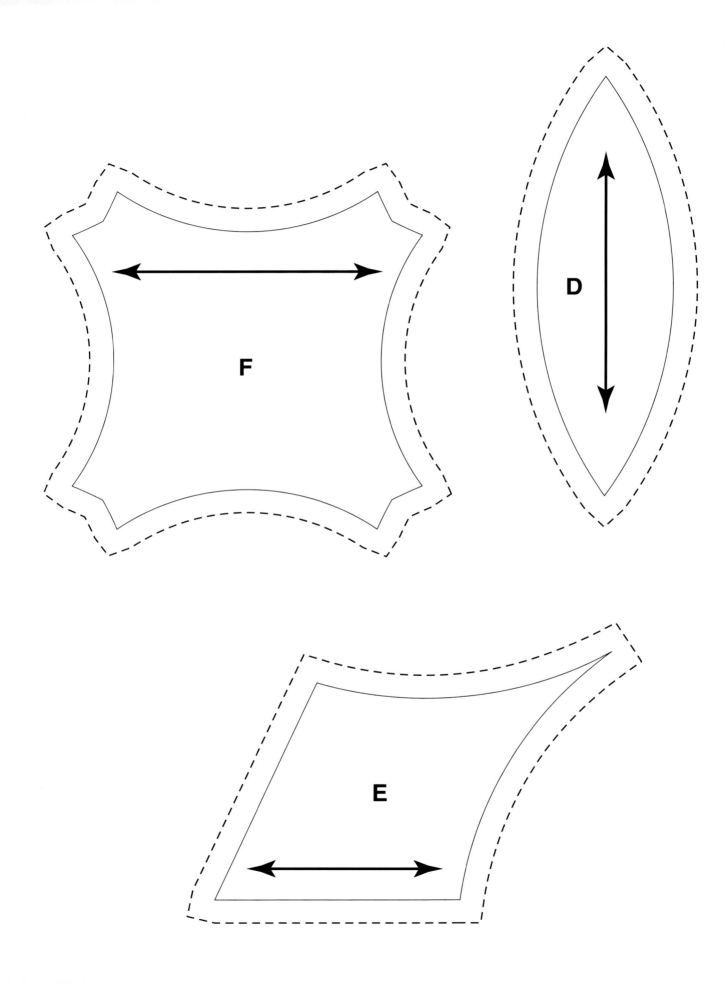

Dutch Tulip

June 23, 1931
12" Block

Fabric needed: white, red, green and gold.

Cut one white 12-1/2" square. Crease the square from corner to corner for positioning purposes.

Trace the pattern pieces onto freezer paper. Pin the pattern pieces to the appropriate color of fabric and cut them out, adding a small seam allowance.

NOTE: *Instead of cutting out a green circle, cut a bias strip and fold it to the same width as the circle and applique it in place. You will have a small connecting seam but the block will be far easier to construct.*

Inset the gold squares into the red half-circles.

Position and pin the pieces to the white fabric and applique in place.

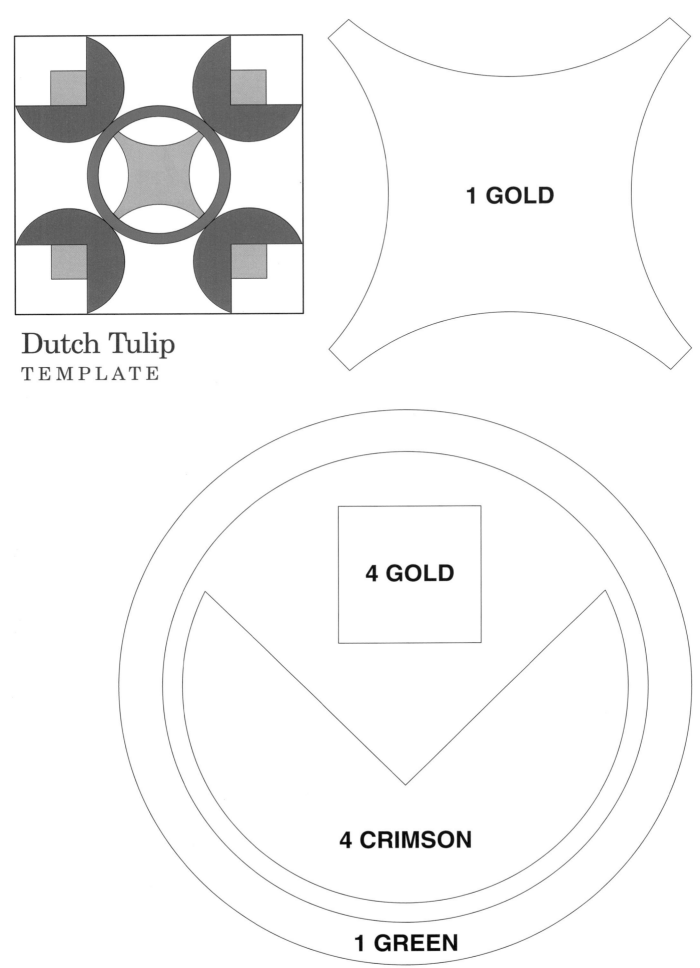

Dutch Tulip
TEMPLATE

1 GOLD

4 GOLD

4 CRIMSON

1 GREEN

Bluebell blocks made by Corky and Peggy Hutinett of Raytown, Mo.

THE
Bluebells

Wild bluebells grow along the roadsides and in the timbers in Illinois. They are shaped a bit different than a bell, having a more elongated flower. Bluebells are sometimes called fairy thimbles.

I hope the fairies are more proficient with their thimbles than I was when I first began to quilt. I made up my mind that I could not use a thimble. As long as I had that mindset, it was true. I started using masking tape on the finger. Those quilting needles are small and pointy and they hurt a lot when one doesn't use a thimble. I soon graduated from masking tape to a leather thimble. I found I could totally tear one of those up in no time flat.

I was looking at quilts at a show in Tennessee and admiring the tiny little stitches. I knew then that I

would never be a good quilter until I learned how to use the correct thimble for the job. Now I slip that (metal) thimble on before I pick up my needle. Funny about that mindset we have and what we can do when we decide it is time to stretch our wings and fly.

Bluebell Applique

**Original Design
By Edie McGinnis
12" Block**

Peggy Hutinett (left) and her cousin Doris Stroh are like sisters. Since Peggy was an only child, Doris was the closest to a sister she had.

Fabric needed: white, blue and green.

Green embroidery floss.

From white fabric, cut a 12-1/2" square.

Trace the bluebell design onto the white fabric for placement purposes.

Trace the pattern onto freezer paper and cut the pieces out of the appropriate color of fabric, adding a small seam allowance.

Pin the pieces to the white square and applique in place.

Embroider the stems of the bluebells and the small caps on the blossoms to complete the block.

Bluebell Applique
TEMPLATE

Bluebell Pieced

January 24, 1940
12" Block

Who Made This Block

Corky Hutinett, married to Peggy, shares in the quilting fun in their household. Corky cuts out fabric for nearly every quilt they make. He enjoys handpiecing, quilting and adding to their considerable fabric stash.

Fabric needed: blue, white and green.

From white fabric, cut out 8 pieces using template B, 4 pieces using template A, 4 pieces using template Ar, 4 pieces using template D, 4 pieces using template F and 4 pieces using template Fr.

From blue fabric, cut 4 pieces using template C and 4 pieces using template Cr.

From green fabric, cut 4 pieces using template E and 4 pieces using template Er and one square using template G.

Sew one white B piece to a blue C piece. Add a white Ar piece as shown.

Sew a white B piece to a blue Cr piece. Add a white A piece as shown.

Sew this segment to the first segment you made. This is the corner (or bluebell) unit. Make 3 more units like this and set aside.

Next we will construct the leaf units by sewing a white F piece to a green Er piece. Then sew a white Fr piece to a green E piece. Sew these to each side of a white D piece. The unit will look like this.

Make 3 more of these leaf units.

To make the top row, sew a corner (bluebell) unit to each side of a leaf unit like this.

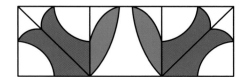

For the middle row, sew a leaf unit to either side of the green square.

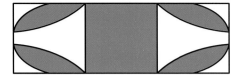

For the bottom row, sew a corner (bluebell) unit to each side of a leaf unit exactly replicating the top row.

Sew the 3 rows together to complete the block.

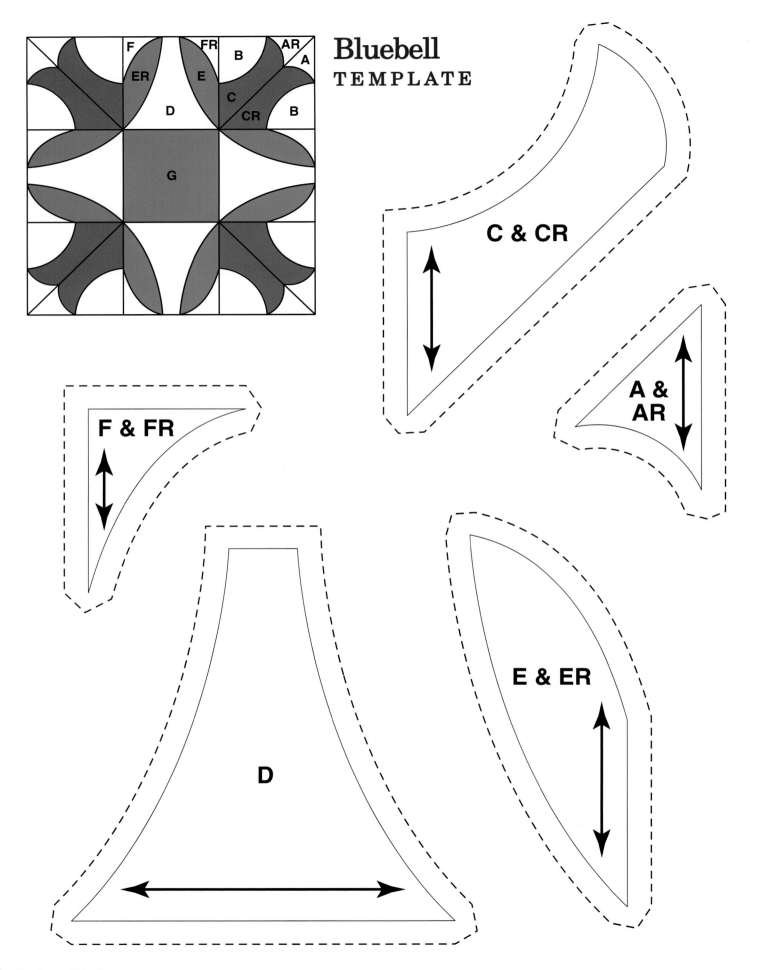

Bluebell
TECHPLATE

Bluebell
TEMPLATE

C & CR

A & AR

F & FR

D

E & ER

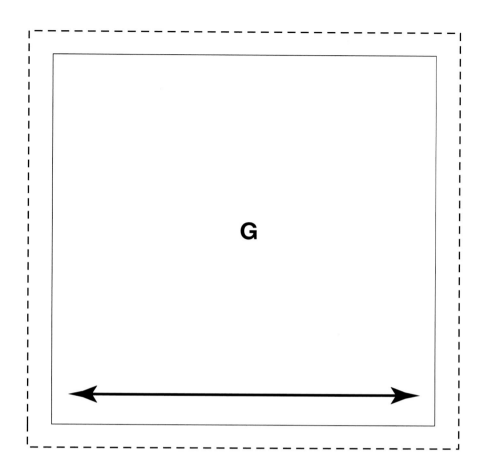

G

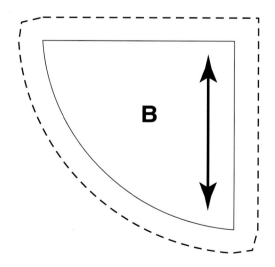

B

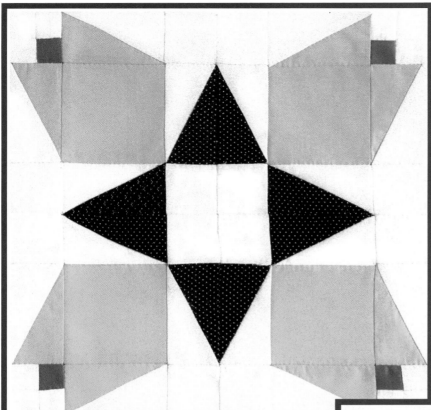

Magnolia Bud and Magnolia Blossom blocks made by Shari McMillan of Marquette Heights, Ill.

THE
Magnolias

When I was twenty, I went to California to visit Ann. She is the lady who gave me my first Siamese cat and the person I dearly love as my second mom.

I arrived in California just as the magnolia tree in Ann's side yard was beginning to bloom. The blossoms were creamy white against their background of waxy, green leaves and had a fragrance that drew hummingbirds out of hiding. Every morning Ann would slip into my bedroom and put a fresh magnolia blossom in the vase on my dresser. It was a wonderful way to start the day.

Magnolia Bud

March 26, 1932
12" Block

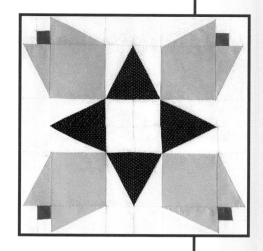

Fabric needed: white, green, pink and rose.

From white fabric, cut 12 squares using template C and 8 triangles using template B, 8 triangles using template Br and 12 squares using template A.

From pink fabric, cut 4 triangles using template B, 4 triangles using template Br, and 4 squares using template D.

From rose fabric, cut 4 squares using template A.

From green fabric, cut 4 triangles using template B and 4 triangles using template Br.

NOTE: *When cutting triangles using template B, your fabric can be folded. This will give you the B reverse pieces needed.*

Sew 2 white A squares together. Then sew 1 white A square to a rose A square making a 4-patch unit that looks like this.

Sew a pink B triangle to a white B triangle. Sew a pink Br triangle to a white Br triangle. You now have two units, each looking like this.

Sew a white B triangle to a green B triangle. Sew a white Br triangle to a green Br triangle. Now you have two units that look like this.

Sew the four-patch unit to a pink and white segment and add a white C square.

Sew the other pink and white segment to the large pink D square. Then add the green and white segment.

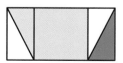

Who Made This Block

Shari McMillan with her sisters Edie McGinnis (left) and Stormy Lee van den Houghten (right). Shari says she and Edie quilt over the phone. Since they live so far from each other they only get to share in person a few times a year. One will describe the block over the phone while the other scrambles for a pencil and paper to draw out what she hears. The telephone quilting bees usually end up in gales of laughter and the problems generally get solved.

Now sew a white C square to each end of
a green and white segment.

Sew the 3 rows together, making a quar-
ter of the block. Make 3 more of these
and sew the 4 pieces together as shown
to complete the block.

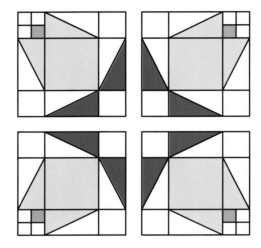

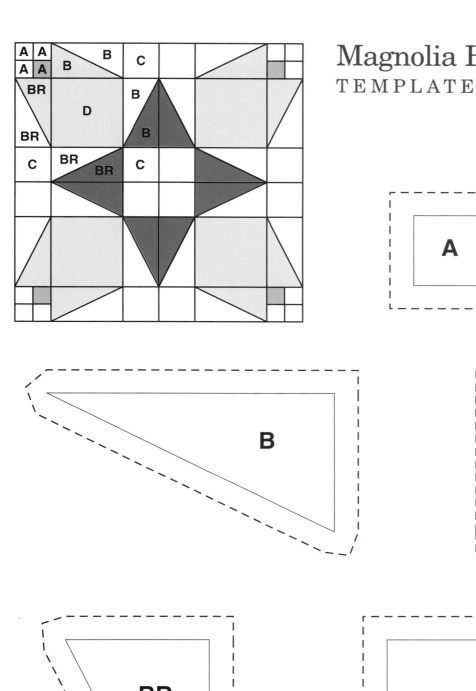

Magnolia Bud
TEMPLATE

A

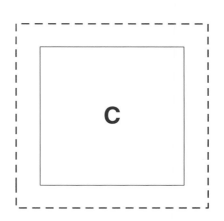
B

C

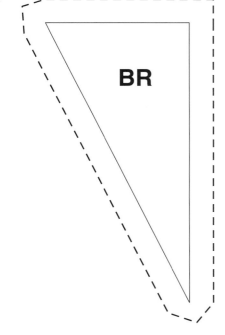
BR

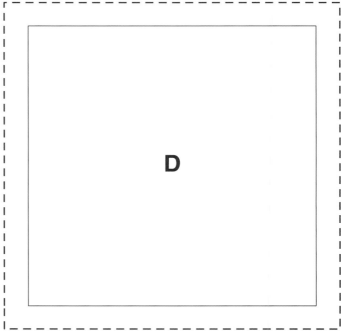
D

Magnolia Applique

**Original Design
By Edie McGinnis
12" Block**

Fabric needed: white, cream, pale yellow, pale green, dark green and brown.

From white fabric, cut a 12-1/2" square. Trace the design onto the fabric for placement purposes.

Trace the design onto freezer paper. Pin the appropriate design to the color of fabric designated in the key on the lower left hand corner of the design. Cut out the applique elements adding a small seam allowance. Pin the pieces in place and applique to complete the block.

Magnolia Applique
TEMPLATE

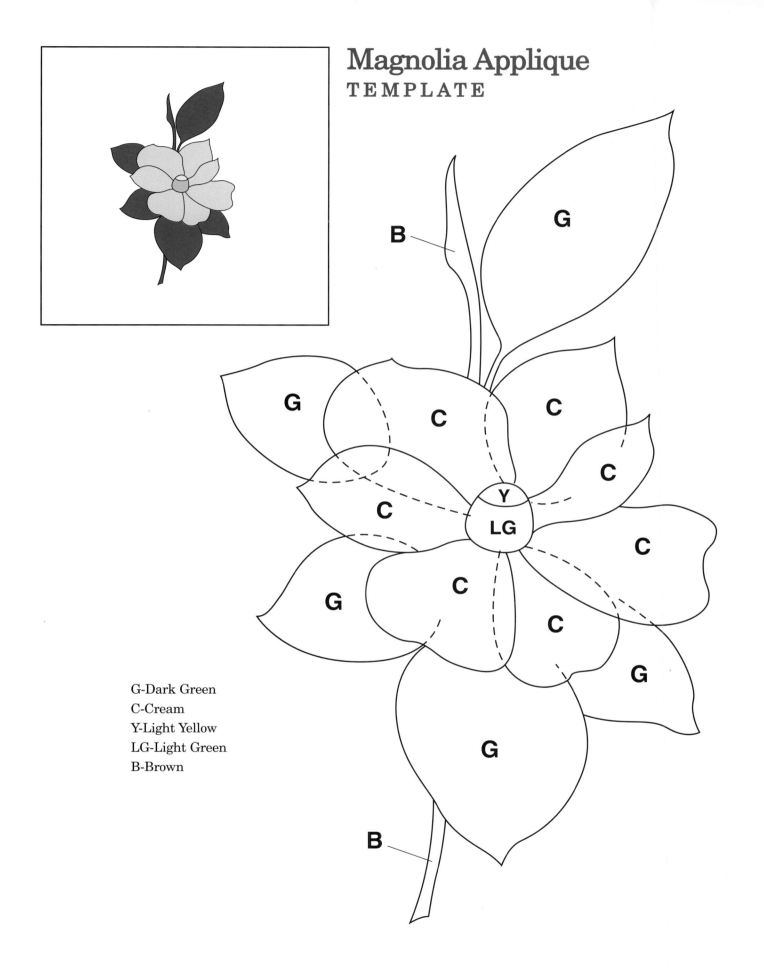

G-Dark Green
C-Cream
Y-Light Yellow
LG-Light Green
B-Brown

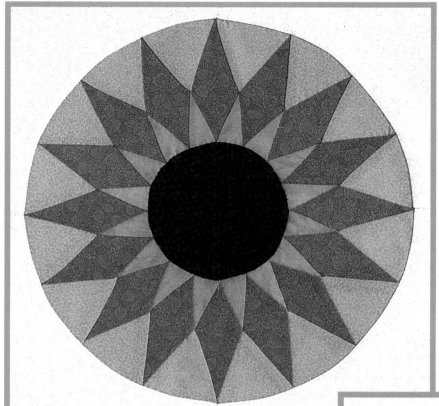

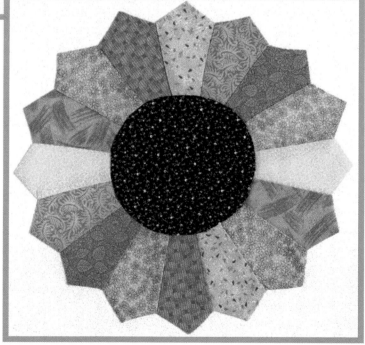

THE *Russian Sunflower* AND THE *Landon* SUNFLOWER

Quilters have been naming quilts after political candidates for a long time. The Landon Sunflower is no exception. The pattern was sent in by Mrs. H. E. Myers of Cherokee, Kan., to mark the campaign being waged for President between Alf Landon and Franklin D. Roosevelt. Landon had won two bids for governor of Kansas and the GOP was hoping he could shake Roosevelt loose from the presidency. In the end, Landon won in only two states, Maine and Vermont.

Alf Landon did leave quite a legacy for Kansas. He got the Kansas legislature to pass a law known as the "cash basis law," which is still on the books. It says that Kansas cannot go into debt and must always have enough money in reserve to meet its budget.

The law was passed during the Depression when the nation first started going into debt.

Landon must have passed on some of his political savvy to his daughter, Nancy Kassebaum. She served the country as a senator from Kansas.

As for that Russian Sunflower, I really don't have a clue where they came up with that name.

Russian Sunflower

May 7, 1932
12" Block

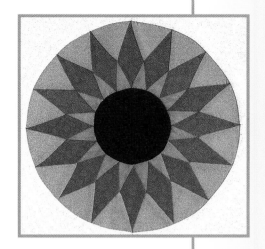

Fabric needed: white, brown, yellow and gold.

From the brown fabric, cut 1 circle using template A.

From the gold fabric, cut 16 diamonds using template B.

From the yellow fabric, cut 16 small triangles using template C and 16 triangles using template D.

From the white fabric, cut 4 pieces using template E. You might want to add a half an inch to the outside of this piece and square the block when you have finished piecing it. The sheer number of pieces in the block and the amount of bias edges can throw it off a bit if one is not totally precise, so squaring the block later can guarantee an accurate finished size of 12-1/2"

Sew a yellow D piece to a gold diamond as shown.

Then add a C triangle.

Add another gold diamond then the D triangle and the C triangle. Continue in this manner until you have used all of the diamonds and triangles. You will have a slightly spiraling strip.

Continued on page 26.

Sew the strip to the brown circle and close the last seam. Your block should look like this.

Add the white E pieces to the outside of the circle, leaving the sides seams open until all the curves are sewn in place. Then sew the side seams closed to complete the block.

Russian Sunflower
TEMPLATE

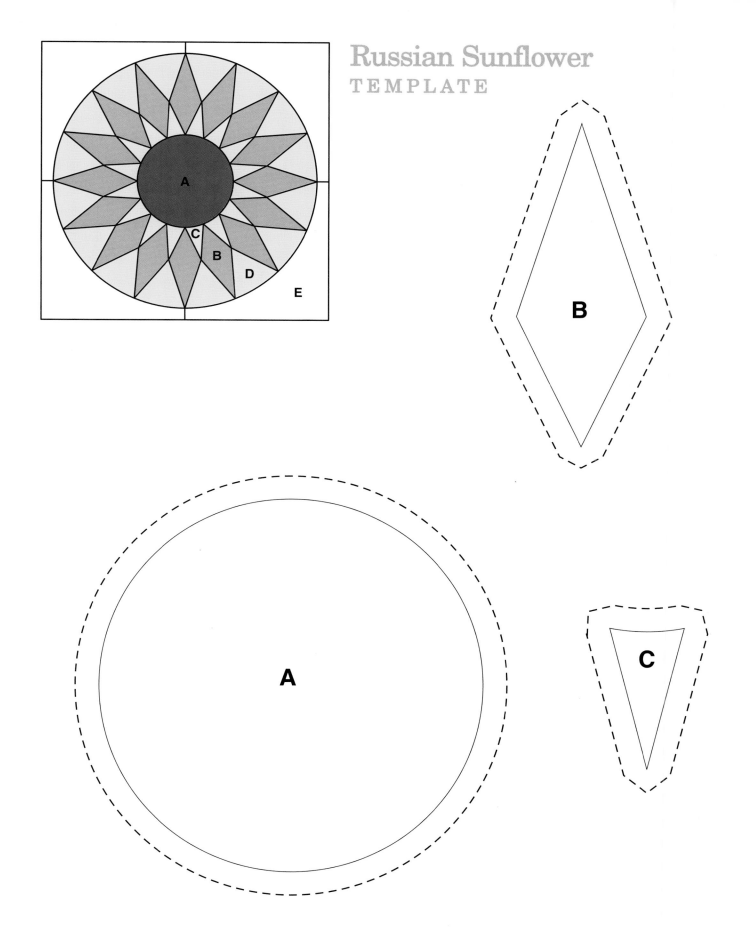

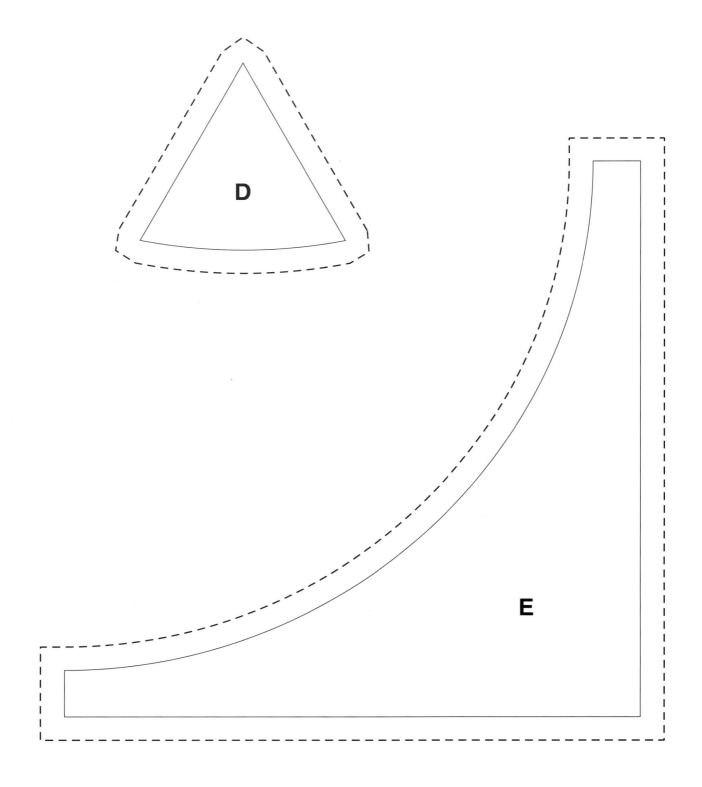

The Landon Sunflower

September 16, 1932
12" Block

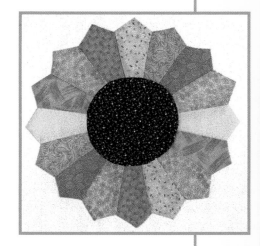

Fabric needed: Brown, gold and white.

From white fabric, cut a 12-1/2" square.

From brown fabric, cut a circle using template A.

From gold fabric, cut 16 petals using template B.

Sew the gold petals together forming a circle.

Fold the white square in fourths and press lightly. Position the ring of petals on the white square, lining up the petals so four of the points match the creases in the white fabric. Applique the petals in place.

Applique the brown circle over the center of the petals. Your block should look like this.

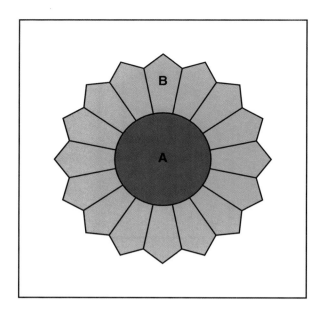

The Landon Sunflower
TEMPLATE

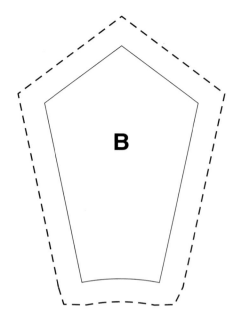

B

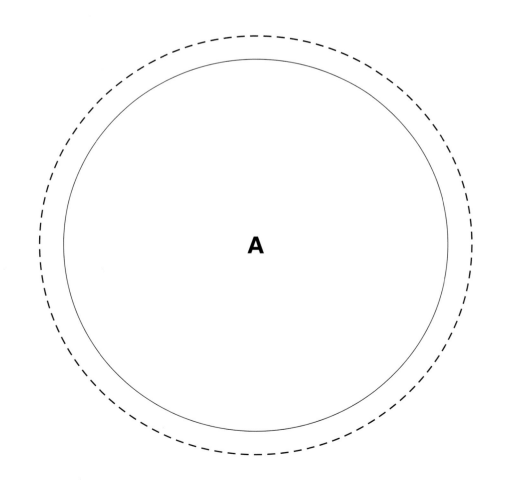

A

Butterfly and June Butterfly blocks made by Barb Maxwell of Pekin, Ill.

THE
Butterflies

We had a lot of flowers around our house and with the flowers came the butterflies. They came in a myriad of colors and sizes. I liked the swallowtails with their vivid coloring, but the monarchs were my favorites. I liked the colors and the sheer number of them one would see when they were migrating. I never understood how their fragile wings could carry them so far.

My dad and I went fishing along the Mackinaw River one day and came upon the Monarchs as they were resting. They covered the fence posts and tree trunks and limbs of bushes. It seemed as though the color orange overwhelmed the area. After drinking in this sight, we left and found another spot to fish. Daddy thought that nothing that glorious should be disturbed.

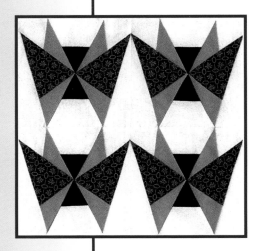

Butterfly

October 17, 1931
12" Block

Who Made This Block

Barbara Maxwell (left) and her sister Cecelia Ash of Pekin, Ill. Barbara says the first quilt class she took was taught by her sister, Cecelia, at JoAnn Fabrics. The quilt was to be a Double Irish Chain but changed to a Triple Irish Chain because she could not bear to get rid of any of the fabrics she had auditioned for the project.

Fabric needed: white, black, print and blue.

From white fabric, cut 8 pieces using template B, 4 pieces using template C, four pieces using template D and 4 pieces using template A.

From black fabric, cut 8 pieces using template F.

From blue fabric, cut 4 pieces using template G, 4 pieces using template H, 4 pieces using template K and 4 pieces using template J.

From print fabric, cut 4 pieces using template I and 4 pieces using template L.

Sew the two white B pieces to the black F pieces.

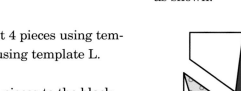

Sew an I print piece to a K blue piece and add a white E piece as shown.

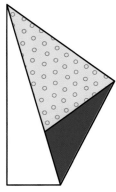

Sew a white A piece to a blue G piece. Sew this to the top of the E-I-K unit as shown.

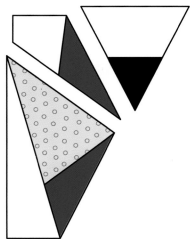

Now add an F-B unit. This makes one-half of the butterfly. To construct the other half of the butterfly, sew a print L piece to a J blue piece. Add a white D piece as shown.

Sew a white C piece to a blue H piece. Sew this to the top of the wing as shown.

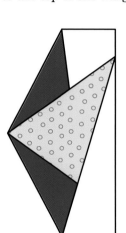

Now sew a B-F unit to this side of the wing. You should now have two sides of the butterfly that look like this.

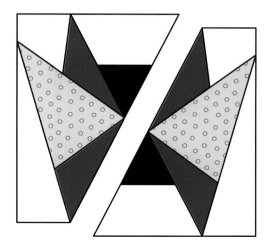

Sew the two halves together to complete one butterfly.

Make three more butterflies.

Sew the four butterflies together to complete the block.

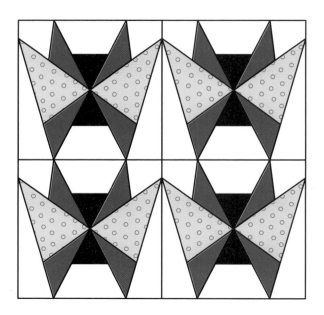

Butterfly
TEMPLATE

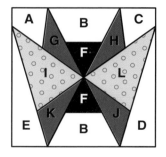

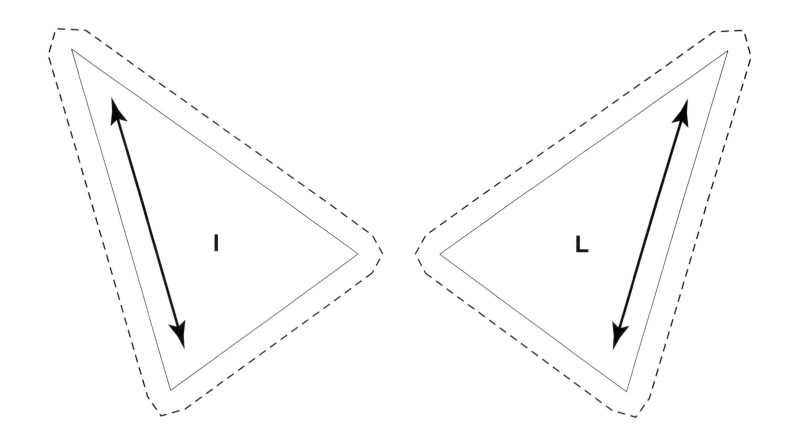

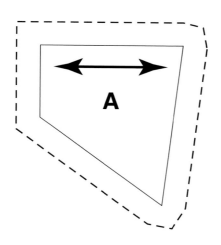

A

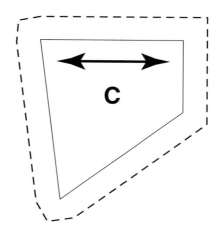

C

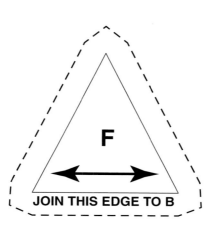

F

JOIN THIS EDGE TO B

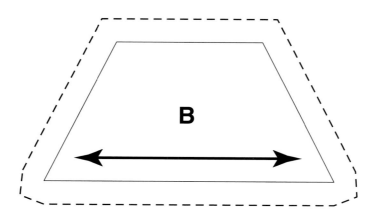

B

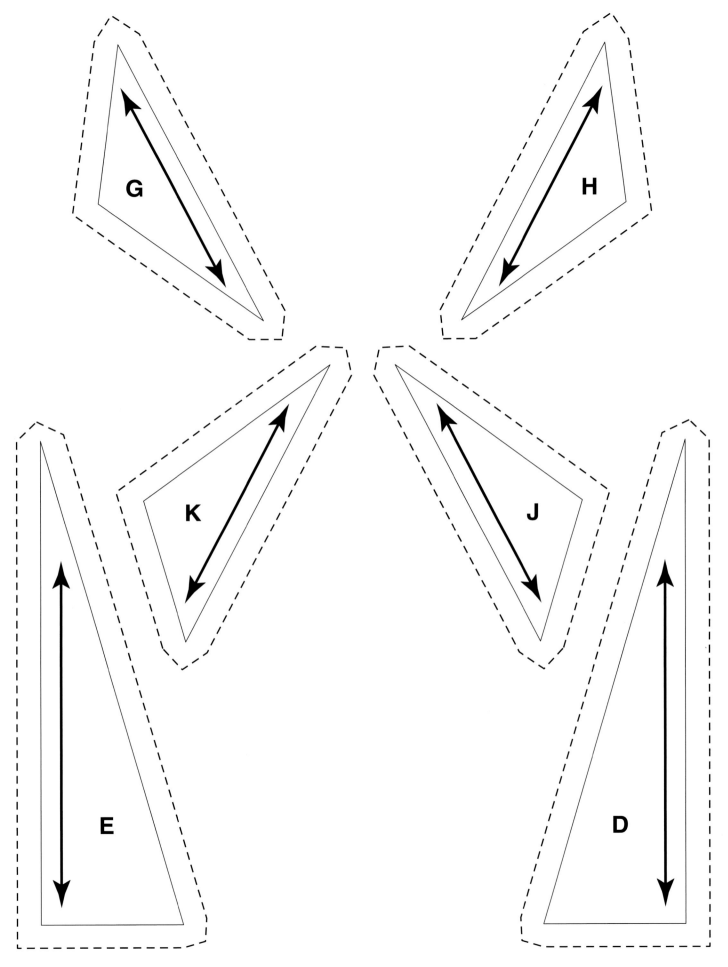

June Butterfly

April 18, 1931
12" Block

Fabric needed: white, medium and dark.

From white fabric cut 2 6-1/2" squares and 2 4-3/4" squares.

From medium fabric, cut 8 triangles using template A.

From dark fabric, cut two butterflies using template B. When cutting out the butterflies, add a small seam allowance.

Sew a triangle to each side of the smaller white square making a diamond in a square. Make two of these units.

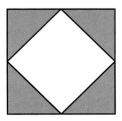

Sew each diamond in a square to a plain white 6-1/2" square. Sew the four squares together as shown.

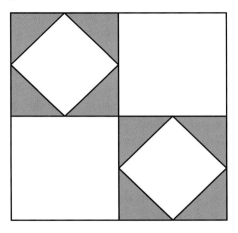

Applique a dark butterfly to each diamond in a square to complete the block.

June Butterfly
TEMPLATE

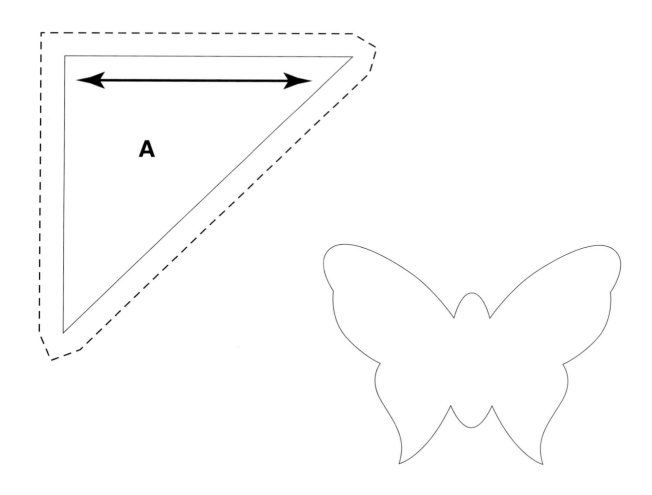

Golden Glow
AND *Gold Bloom*

When the winds blew hot and the humidity climbed during the summer, the Black Eyed Susans thrived. They were along the roadside decorating the fence rows and brightening up the Burma Shave signs. The yellow of those flowers could still be seen through the dust that passing cars churned up and layered on the petals.

A bouquet of Queen Anne's Lace and Black Eyed Susans frequently decorated our kitchen table. I always thought the flowers looked almost as good sitting on that table as the Sunday meal of fried chicken did. Almost.

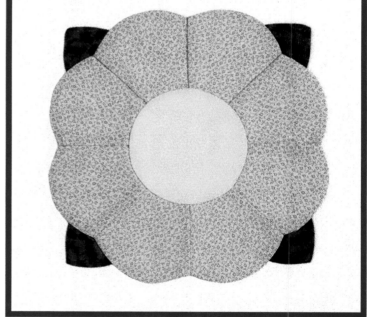

Golden Glow

August 13, 1932
12" Block

Who Made This Block

From left to right are Linda Hilyer and her big sister Peggy McFeeters. Peggy says she and her sister are very different in many ways. In sewing they found ways to make those differences work together. One Friday evening Peggy and Linda were sewing culottes and a vest together. Linda pinned and ran the sewing machine; Peggy cut the fabric and did the handwork. They complimented each other in the team effort.

Fabric needed: white, gold and brown.

From the white fabric, cut 4 squares using template A, 4 triangles using template B and 8 pieces using template C.

From the gold fabric, cut 8 pieces using template D.

From the brown fabric, cut 1 circle using template E.

Sew the white C pieces to the gold D pieces as shown. The C pieces will need to be eased in place. These pieces will puff up as they will be slightly gathered. A gathering stitch can be run all the way around this piece and pulled until the piece fits to simplify the process.

Sew all the C and D pieces together until you have a strip. Sew the strip onto the brown circle. Ease the petals as needed and close the last seam.

Inset the corner squares and the triangles to complete the block.

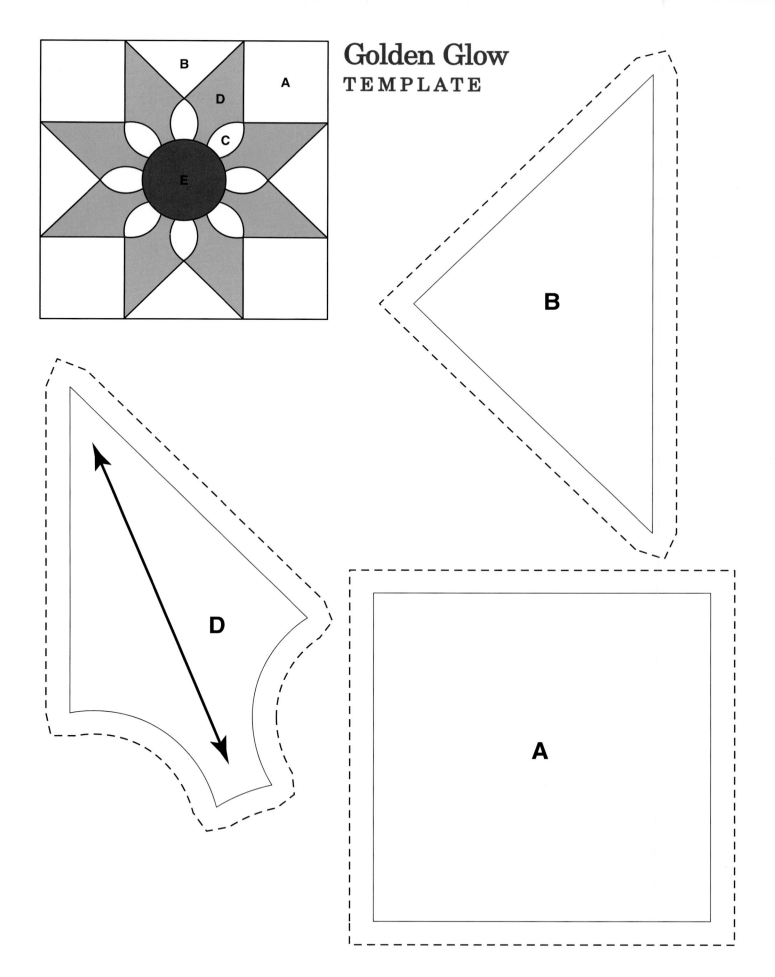

Golden Glow
TEMPLATE

B

D

A

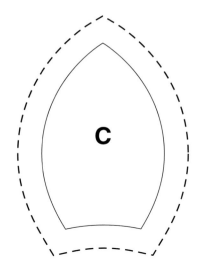

C

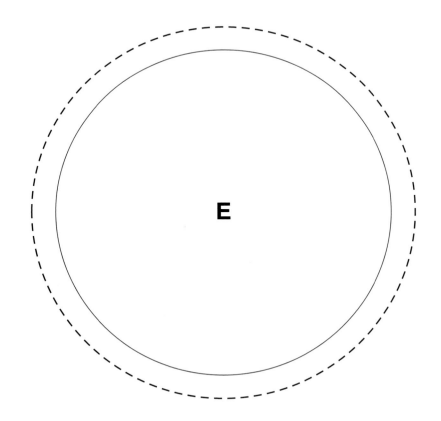

E

Gold Bloom

September 4, 1935
12" Block

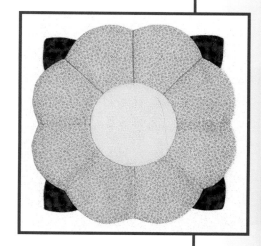

Fabric needed: white, green, yellow and gold.

From white fabric, cut 1 12-1/2" white square. Fold the square from corner to corner and press the creases in for placement purposes. The green leaves should line up with the creases.

From green fabric, cut 4 leaves using template A.

From yellow fabric, cut 1 circle using template C.

From gold fabric, cut 8 petals using template B.

Sew the 8 petals together. You will have a ring when finished. Applique the yellow circle to the center of the flower.

Position the flower and the green leaves on the white block and applique in place to complete the block.

Gold Bloom
TEMPLATE

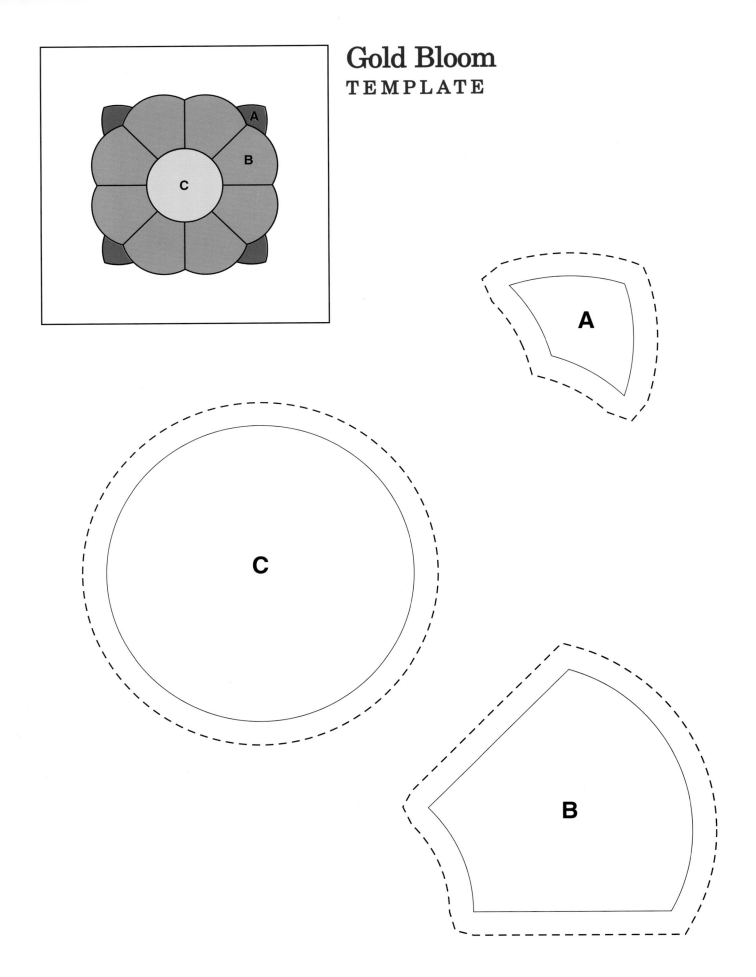

A

C

B

Franklin D. Roosevelt block appliqued by Ruth Lofgren of Fort Leavenworth, Kan.

President Roosevelt AND FRANKLIN D. *Roosevelt*

Franklin D. Roosevelt, elected to the White House for four terms, was a much-loved president. He was stricken in 1921 with polio, a disease that could have compromised his budding political career.

In 1924 he discovered the curative powers of the hot springs in Warm Springs, Ga. He swam daily in the springs and grew stronger and healthier and more enthusiastic about his life and career. In 1928 he was elected governor of New York and then became the Democratic nominee for president in 1932. It was the beginning of the longest rule of the White House by one man.

Roosevelt made Warm Springs his retreat while in office. He established The Warm Springs Foundation dedicated to helping people who also suffered from polio. He held "Birthday Balls" to raise money for the Foundation. The balls were the forerunners of the March of Dimes program.

With the advent of the Salk vaccine in 1954, polio was eradicated. The foundation eventually became the Roosevelt Warm Springs Institute for Rehabilitation and today serves as a rehab facility for people with paralytic and orthopedic disorders, victims of stroke,

Continued on page 46.

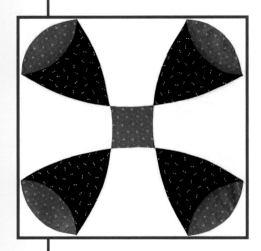

President Roosevelt

May 17, 1944
12" block

amputation, brain injuries, etc.

Quiltmakers have been recording history in their quilts since people began to make quilts. The Franklin D. Roosevelt block was a result of a nationwide celebration of Roosevelt's birthday in 1934. The block called attention to his Warm Springs Foundation and the restorative cures the Springs offered. Interestingly enough, the Star printed the pattern with the lettering for the flag and the words "Franklin D. Roosevelt" but neglected to print the words "Warm Springs Foundation for Good Health" as shown on the icon that portrayed the finished block. I guess The Star just expected the quilter to add that piece of information herself.

Fabric needed: red, white and blue.

From red fabric, cut 1 piece using template A and four ovals using template B.

From blue fabric, cut 4 pieces using template C.

From the white fabric, cut 4 pieces using template D and 4 corner pieces using template E.

Sew one white E corner piece to one red B oval. Sew this to a blue C piece making a unit that looks like this.

Make three more of these bell shaped units. Then sew a bell unit to each side of a white D piece. Do this twice so you have two segments that look like this.

Sew a white D piece to each side of the red square making a segment that looks like this.

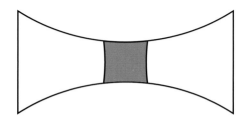

Now sew the three segments together to complete the block. It will look like this.

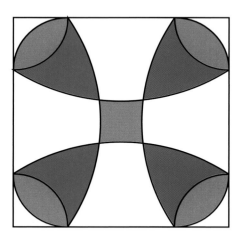

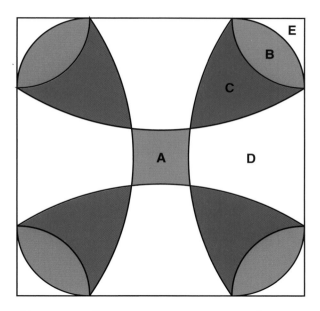

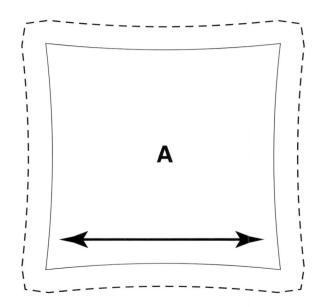

President Roosevelt
TEMPLATE

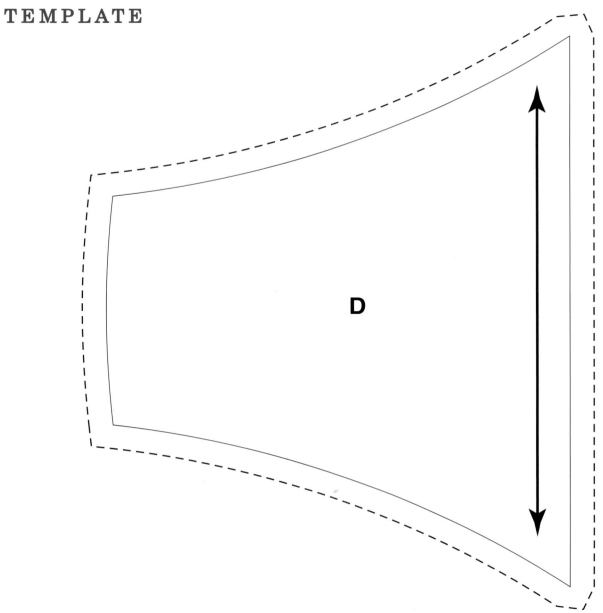

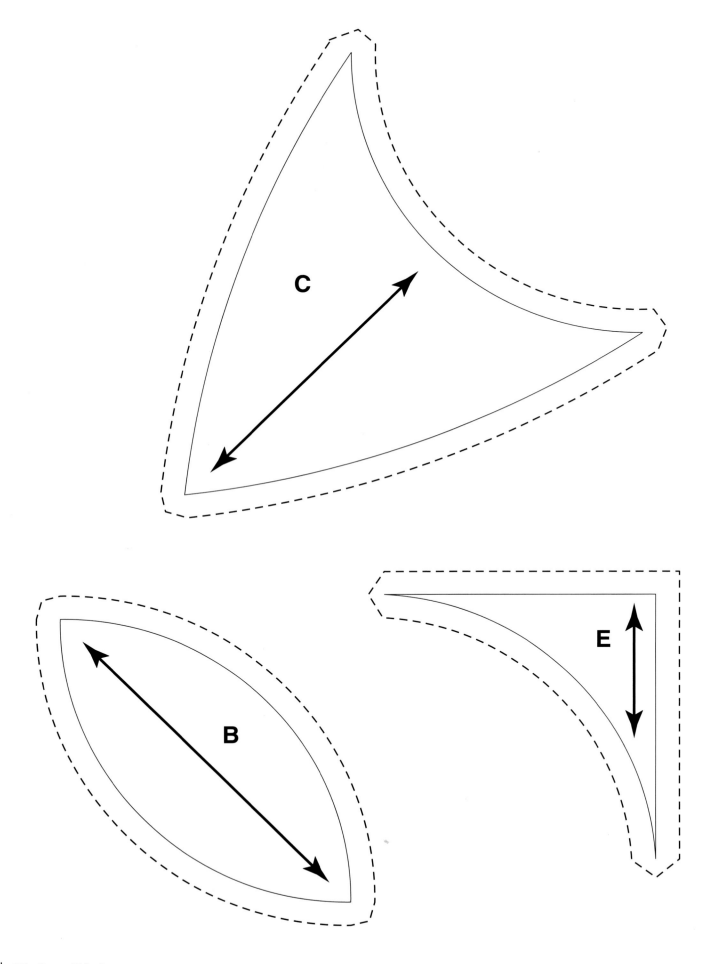

Franklin D. Roosevelt

January 27, 1934
12" Block

Fabric needed: red, white and blue.

White and blue embroidery floss.

From the red fabric, cut 2 strips 2" by 12-1/2" and one flag.

From the white fabric, cut 2 strips 2" by 12-1/2" and two white stars and one monument.

From the blue fabric, cut 1 rectangle 6-1/2" by 12-1/2"

Trace the lettering onto the appropriate fabric. Sew the red and the white strips together. Sew one set of strips to the top of the blue rectangle. Applique the monument then sew the remaining set of strips to the bottom of the blue rectangle. Your block should look like this.

Applique the stars and flag to the block. Either embroider the words and flag pole or use an indelible pen to complete the block.

Ruth Kelley Lofgren and sister Joyce Kelley in Quincy, Ill., were dressed alike in this photo. They were often asked if they were twins. Their family referred to them as "the Kelley girls." As children, Joyce loved to cook and Ruth loved to sew. Joyce now works in the food industry and Ruth works in a quilt shop and teaches quilting.

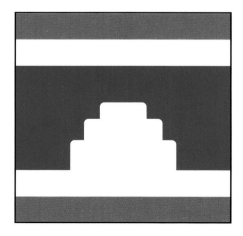

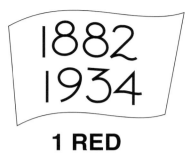

Franklin D. Roosevelt
TEMPLATE

1882
1934

1 RED

ROOSEVELT

FRANKLIN D

2 WHITE

WARM

SPRINGS

FOUNDATION

FOR GOOD HEALTH

The Quilt Gallery

As we quilters all know, there is nothing quite like a quilt show to get our creativity activated. It is where we go to look, learn, get ideas, compare our level of ability and, if we are lucky, spend our money at a merchant's mall. It is where we meet with our sister quilters and drool over all the lovely, finished quilts. It is where we go to whine and grimace and wish we had finished the quilt that we had left at home at some unfinished stage or another. A quilt show represents a goal and a chance to be recognized for our talent and our skill. It is also an opportunity to dream about and plan our next project.

Step into our quilt show on the following pages and dream and drool and plan at your leisure. Some talented quilters and a devout collector are sharing their beautiful quilts with us. Enjoy yourself.

A Century Old Tulip

A Century Old Tulip quilt owned by Judy Streu
of Liberty, Mo.

Golden Glow

Courtney Fiser is wrapped up in her Golden Glow quilt that was made by Caroline "Aunt Carrie" Oehmke in the late '30s. Courtney received the quilt from her great-grandma Oehmke, Carrie's sister-in-law.

Flower of Spring

Flower of Spring quilts owned by Lynn Kennedy of Liberty, Mo. The quilts are twin size and were purchased in Oklahoma and are mirror images of each other. Wrapped in the quilts are Jessica and Morgan Elliott of Independence, Mo.

Four Leaf Clover

Four Leaf Clover quilt owned by Nancy Dietz of Lenexa, Kan. The quilt is hand pieced and was purchased in 1985 in St. Joseph, Mo. Nancy hand quilted this top to turn it into a finished quilt in 1986.

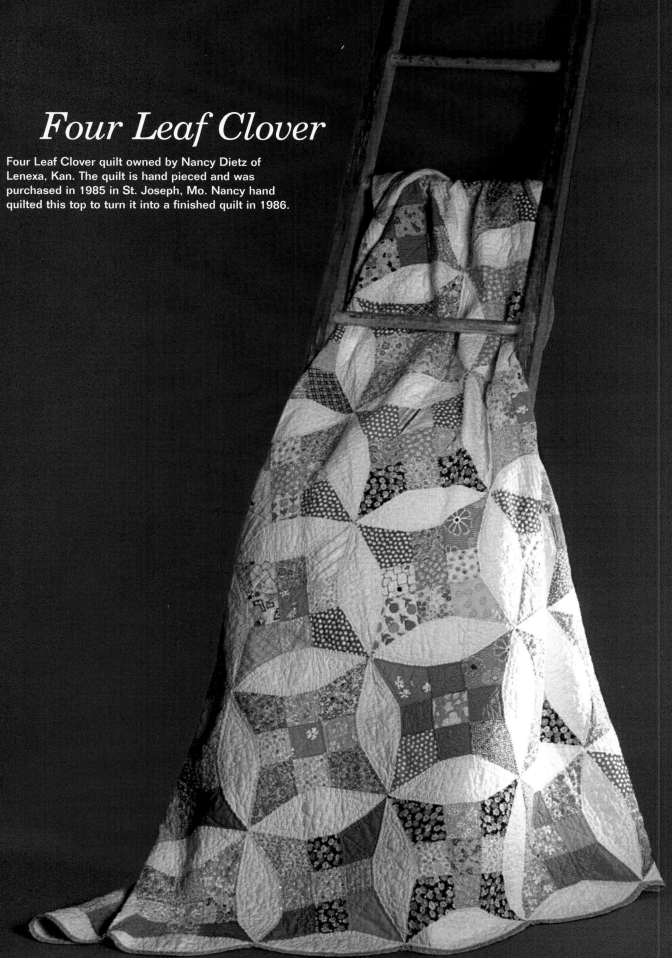

Four Leaf Clover

Four Leaf Clover quilt owned by Ruth Lofgren of Ft. Leavenworth, Kan. The quilt was purchased at an estate sale in Leavenworth, Kan.

Golden Glow

Golden Glow quilt made and owned
by Josie Riner of Shawnee, Kan.

Kite Quilt

Kite Quilt owned by Ruth Lofgren of Ft. Leavenworth, Kan. The quilt is hand pieced and hand quilted. The quilt was purchased at an estate sale.

Kite Quilt

Kite Quilt owned by Judy Streu of Liberty, Mo.

Landon Sunflower

Landon Sunflower quilt owned by
Judy Streu of Liberty, Mo.

Rose Cross

Rose Cross quilt owned by
Judy Streu of Liberty, Mo.

Russian Sunflower

Russian Sunflower quilt owned by
Judy Streu of Liberty, Mo.

Sampler Quilt

Sampler quilt made in the '30s by Mrs. R. E. De Lancy from patterns printed in The Kansas City Star. The quilt is owned by her granddaughter, Gayle Buckley Carlton.

Hickory Leaf or Order No. 11 appliqued by Mary Ellen Bloomquist of Independence, Mo.

Hickory Leaf block pieced by Arlene Johnson of Kansas City, Mo.

Order No. 11
AND *Hickory Leaf*

I have always been a history buff. I grew up in Illinois, The Land of Lincoln. My grade school teachers made sure we knew about "Old Abe." Our education was not complete without a trip to visit Lincoln's home, the capital building and Lincoln's tomb (both the old and the new). One of the kids with whom I went to school had a large family and they lived in what had once been a hotel. Rumor had it that Lincoln stayed there when he was riding circuit.

About the time I was 16, I went to a Civil War battle-field just over the border from Tennessee into Georgia. I noticed that most of the monuments were dedicated to Northern troops. I thought that was a bit odd so I asked the lady who was giving tours why there were no monuments for the Southern soldiers.

She haughtily replied, "Well, you just shoveled our men into trenches." I was thinking that I had absolutely nothing to do with it since that had happened about 80 years before I had been born.

Now I live in Missouri and I recently learned of Order No. 11 issued by Gen. Thomas Ewing. The

Continued on page 65.

Hickory Leaf or Order No. 11

November 23, 1929
12" Block

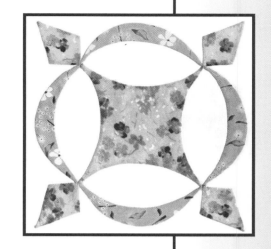

Fabric needed: white, peach and yellow.

From white fabric, cut one 12-1/2" square.

From yellow fabric, cut 1 piece using template A and 4 pieces using template B.

From peach fabric, cut 4 pieces using template C.

Pin pieces to white fabric and applique in place.

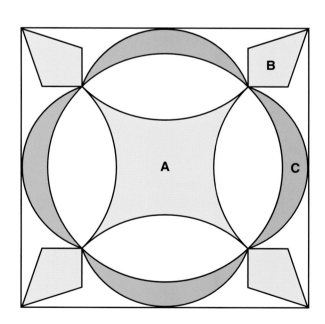

From page 64.

consequence of this order was to evict people living in the counties of Bates, Jackson, Cass and part of Vernon. They had 15 days to prove their loyalty to the Union or get out, leaving all of their possessions behind. The Union soldiers arrived before the time limit had expired and began to kill the residents and loot their homes.

According to The Kansas City Star, a 10-year-old girl named Fannie Kreeger Haller saw her mother's lovely new quilt stolen off of the bed by looters. The quilt had been made from the Hickory Leaf applique pattern. Fannie carried the pattern in her mind and reproduced the quilt as an adult and called it Order No. 11.

Hickory Leaf or Order No. 11
TEMPLATE

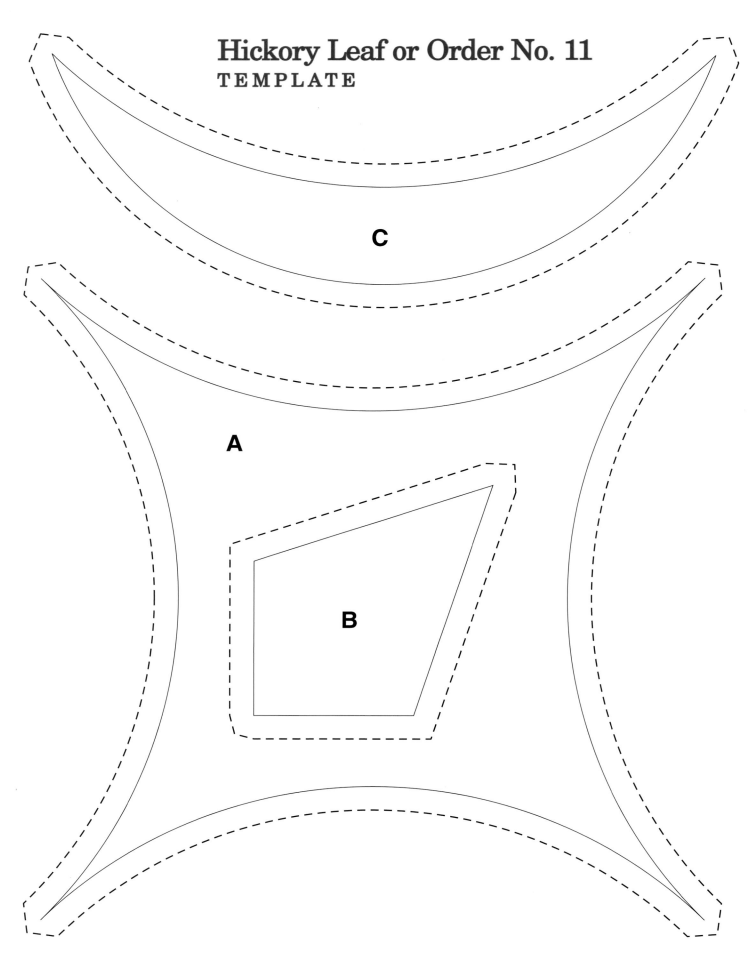

C

A

B

Hickory Leaf

**Original Design
by Edie McGinnis
12" Block**

Fabric needed: white and brown.

From white fabric, cut 5 2-7/8" squares, 2 triangles using template A, 2 triangles using template B and 2 triangles using template D.

From brown fabric, cut 5 2-7/8" squares, 2 triangles using template C, 1 square using template F and 1 stem using template E.

Place each white 2-7/8" square on top of a brown 2-7/8" square. Draw a line from corner to corner on the white square and sew 1/4" on each side of the line. Cut along the line, open each square and press toward the dark side of the fabric. These are called half-square triangle units. (You will have one unit left over.)

Sew the half-square triangle units together as shown.

Sew 3 half-square triangle units together as shown.

Sew one white triangle to the end of one of the half-square triangle segments and add a brown C triangle. Then sew a white A triangle to this making the top left corner of the block as shown.

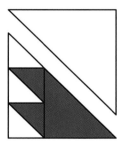

Now sew a half-square triangle segment to the top of the brown F square and add the three half-square triangle segments.

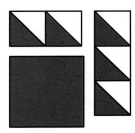

Sew these two quarters of the block together.

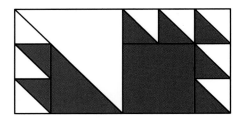

To make the lower left corner of the block, sew a D white triangle to each side of the brown E stem.

To make the lower right corner of the block, sew the remaining white B triangle to the last half-square triangle segment. Sew this to a brown C triangle and add a white A triangle as shown.

Sew the stem unit to the segment you
have just finished.

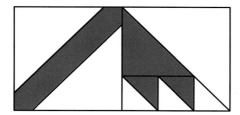

Sew the two rows together to complete
the block. It should look like this.

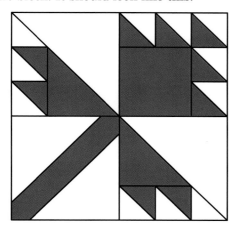

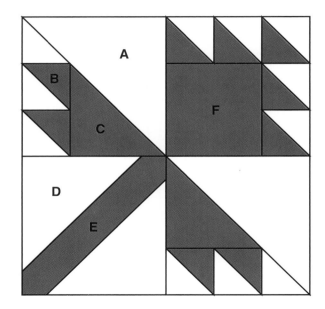

Hickory Leaf
TEMPLATE

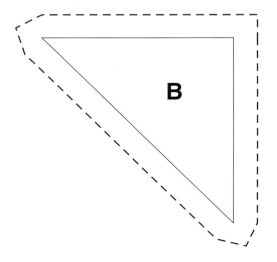

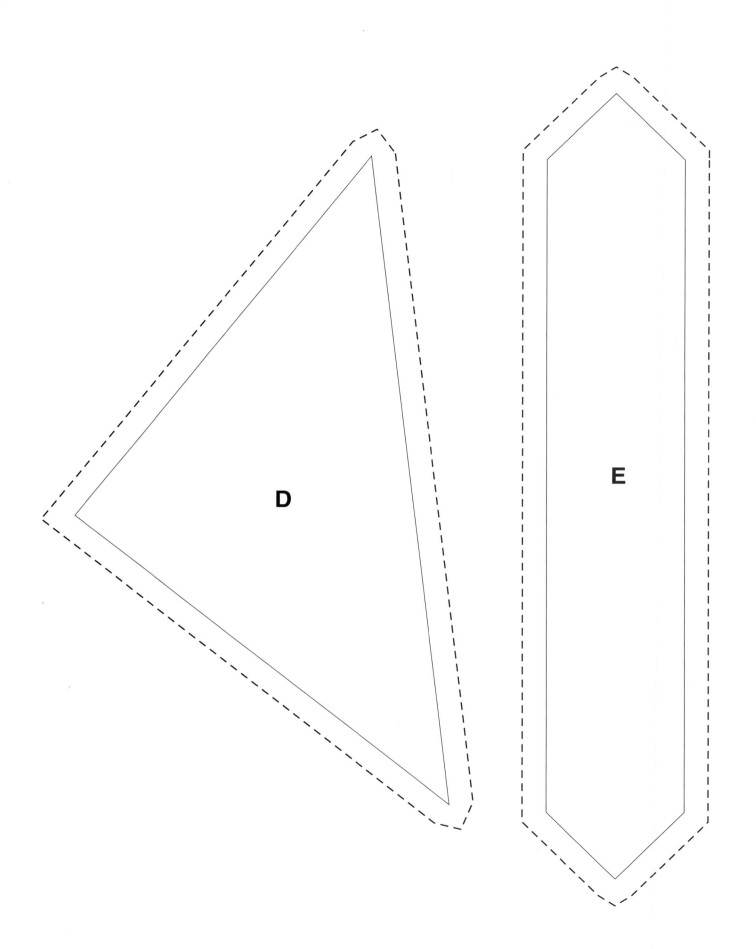

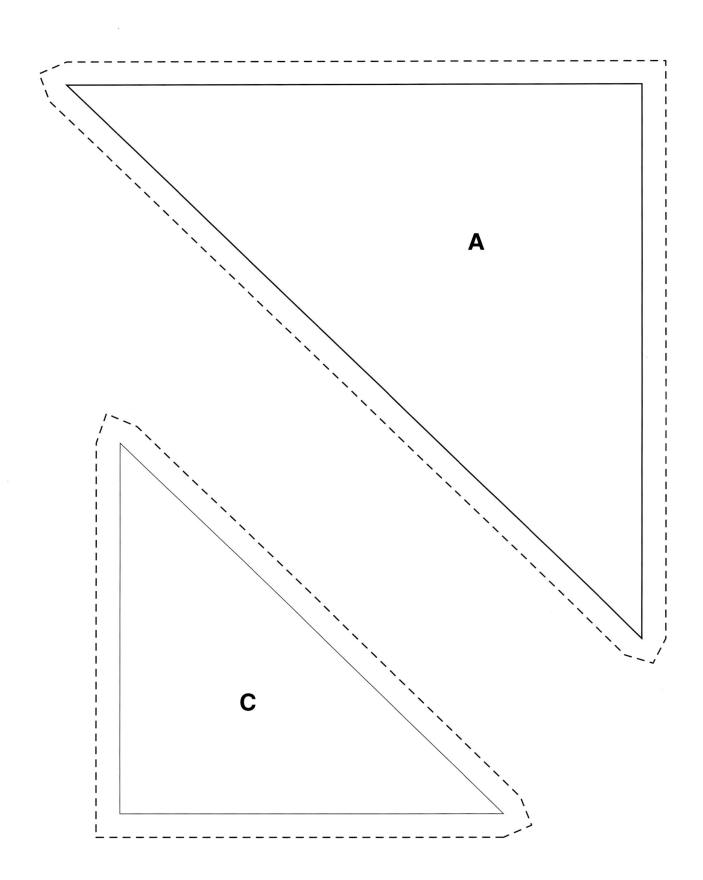

A

C

Kite blocks made by Debbie Pulley
of Peoria, Ill.

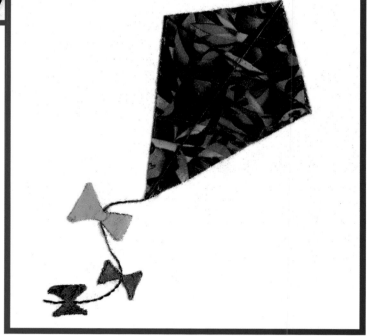

THE *Kites*

When I was about 10 years old, we had a very long, cold and snowy winter. The television was broken and we were feeling very house bound and bored by February. My dad came up with the idea of making a kite, since spring would soon arrive. Not only would we make a kite, we would make a big kite, a 6-foot-tall kite.

Out came the flour and water paste and the newspapers. We glued and glued and glued. Daddy made the crossbows for the kite and put the string around the frame. We cut and glued our newspaper base to the frame and waited for spring to arrive. While we waited, we bragged about our big kite to the other kids in the neighborhood. They said the kite would never fly.

Well, we knew it would. Our dad had said it would. Since we knew he had not only hung the moon but the stars as well, he had to be right. I bet my Roy

Rogers cap gun and holster on my dad and the big kite against the skeptic's bag of marbles.

March came and with it the winds. We got the kite out of the shed and used clothesline rope for string. On the first try the kite twisted up momentarily and thunked to the ground. We needed a tail. A very long tail.

Continued on page 74.

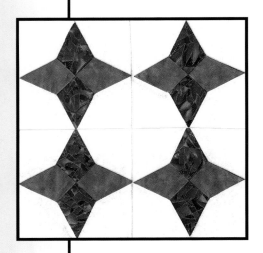

The Kite Quilt Pieced

June 27, 1931
12" Block

From page 73.

The tail was attached and the kite sailed into the air and stayed there. I held out my hand to the neighbor kid and he placed a bag of marbles in it without uttering a word of protest.

Fabric needed: dark, medium and white.

From white fabric, cut 16 pieces using template A.

From medium fabric, cut 8 pieces using template B.

From dark fabric, cut 8 pieces using template B.

Sew a medium B piece to a dark B piece. Make 8 of these units.

Sew two units together making a 4-pointed star. Add an A piece to each star corner as shown.

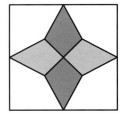

Make three more of these sub blocks and sew the four together to finish the block as shown.

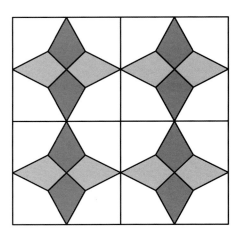

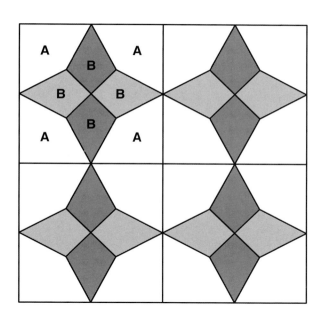

The Kites
TEMPLATE

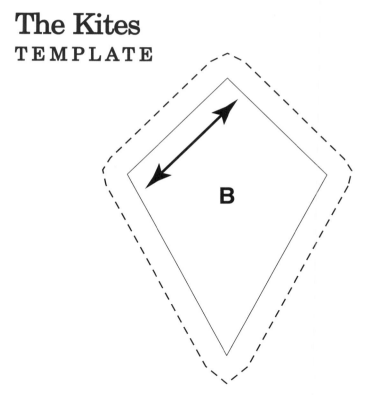

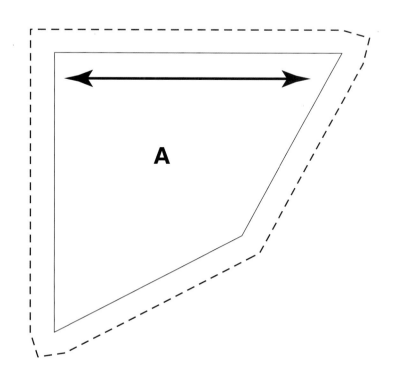

Kite Quilt Applique

**Original Design
By Edie McGinnis
12" Block**

Fabric needed: White and scraps.

Gray embroidery thread for tail.

From white fabric, cut a 12-1/2" square.

Trace the kite and tail onto white fabric
for positioning purposes. Trace the
pattern onto freezer paper and cut the
kite and tail pieces out of brightly colored
scraps. Applique in place.

Embroider the string of the tail with
the gray embroidery floss to complete
the block.

The Kites Applique
TEMPLATE

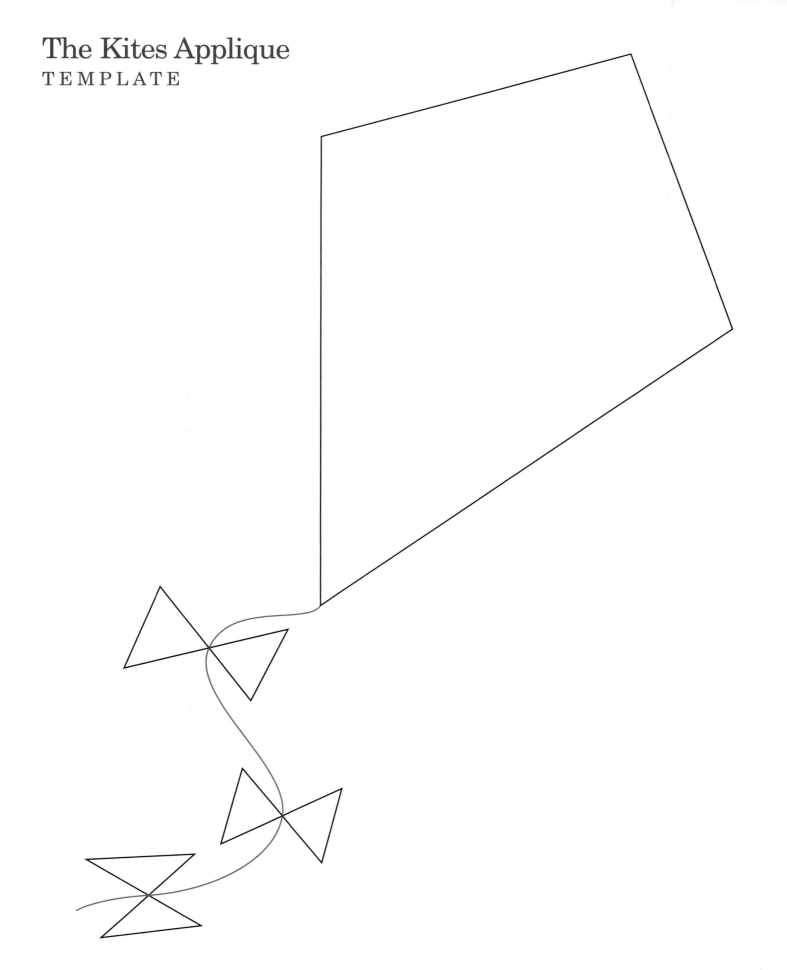

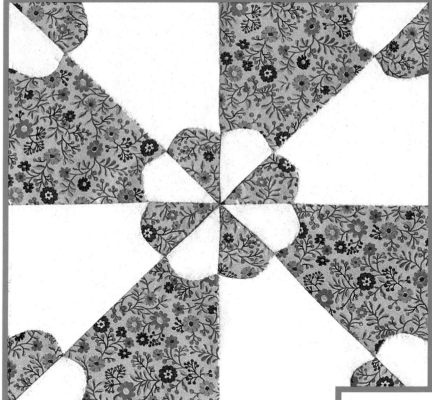

Springtime Blossoms and Flower of Spring blocks made by Cecelia Ash of Pekin, Ill.

Springtime Blossoms AND Flower OF Spring

My grandma's porch was where we all congregated to visit. We would sit in the old porch swing and chat, shell peas and snap green beans. Sometimes we just snuggled with her because she was such a comforting person.

The porch was surrounded by flowers and blooming bushes. The mix of fragrances was breathtaking at times. I liked standing on the steps in the spring and seeing the leaves greening up and then the blossoms emerging. My grandma enjoyed it too. She would stand there with her arm around my shoulders and look at the progress of Mother Nature. There was

always the grandest look of contentment on her face when she was still like that.

Springtime Blossoms

July 20, 1929
12" Block

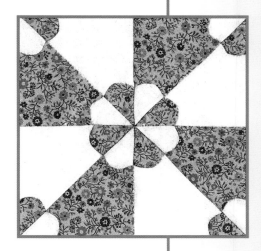

Fabric needed: white and print.

From the white fabric, cut 4 pieces using template B and 4 pieces using template A and 4 pieces using template E.

From the print fabric, cut 4 pieces using template C and 4 pieces using template D and 4 pieces using template F.

Sew a print A piece to a white B piece. Then add a print E piece.

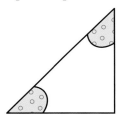

Sew a white F piece to a print C piece and add a white D piece as shown.

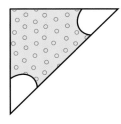

Join these two triangles together making a square that looks like this.

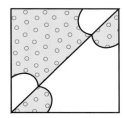

Make three more of these units and sew the units together as shown to complete your block.

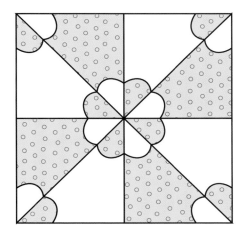

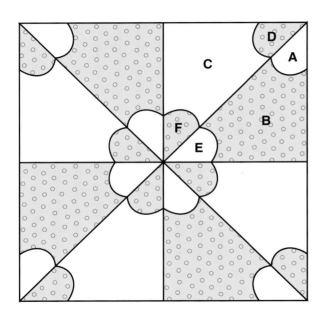

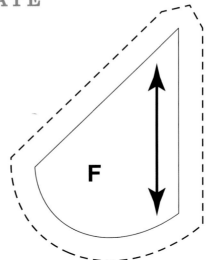

F

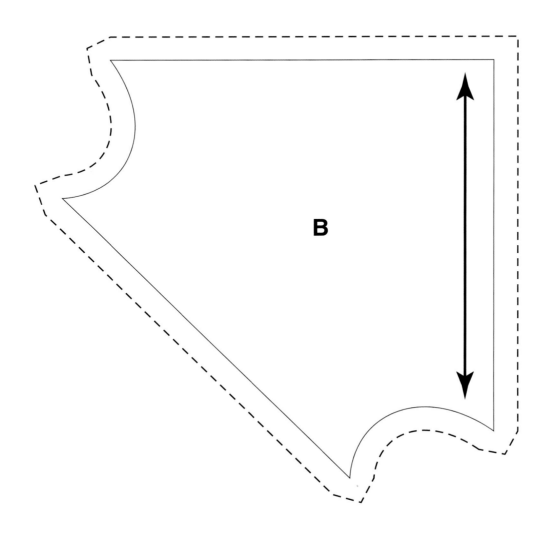

B

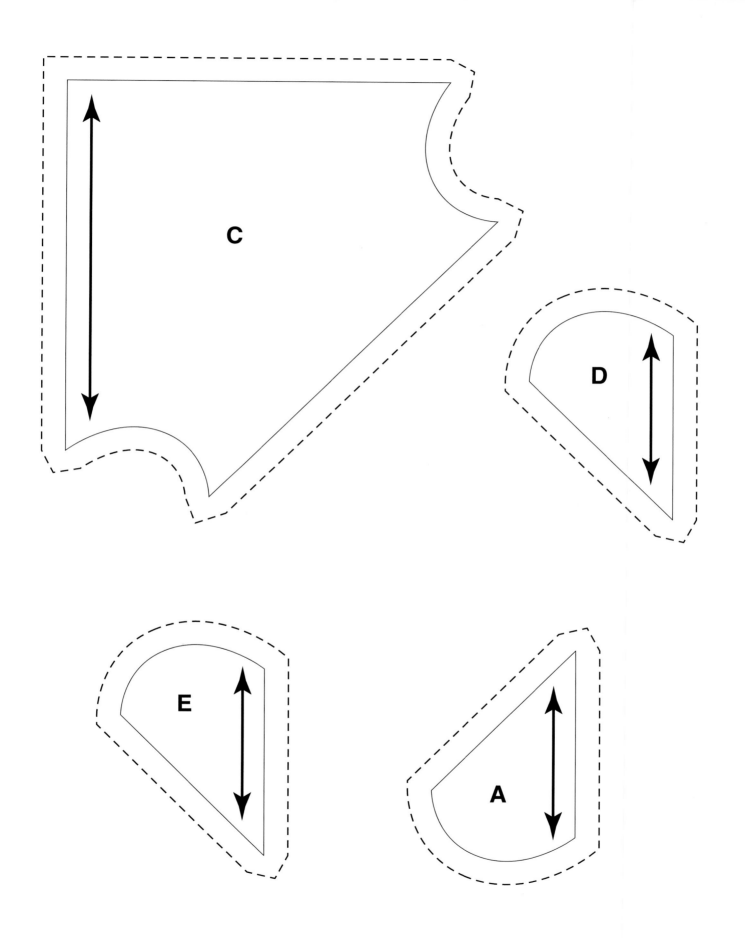

Flower of Spring

January 11, 1936
12" Block

Fabric needed: white, green, rose, orange or peach.

From white fabric, cut one 12-1/2" square.

Trace the pattern pieces onto freezer paper. Pin the paper to the appropriate color of fabric and cut the pieces, adding a small seam allowance. Pin the pieces to the white square and applique in place.

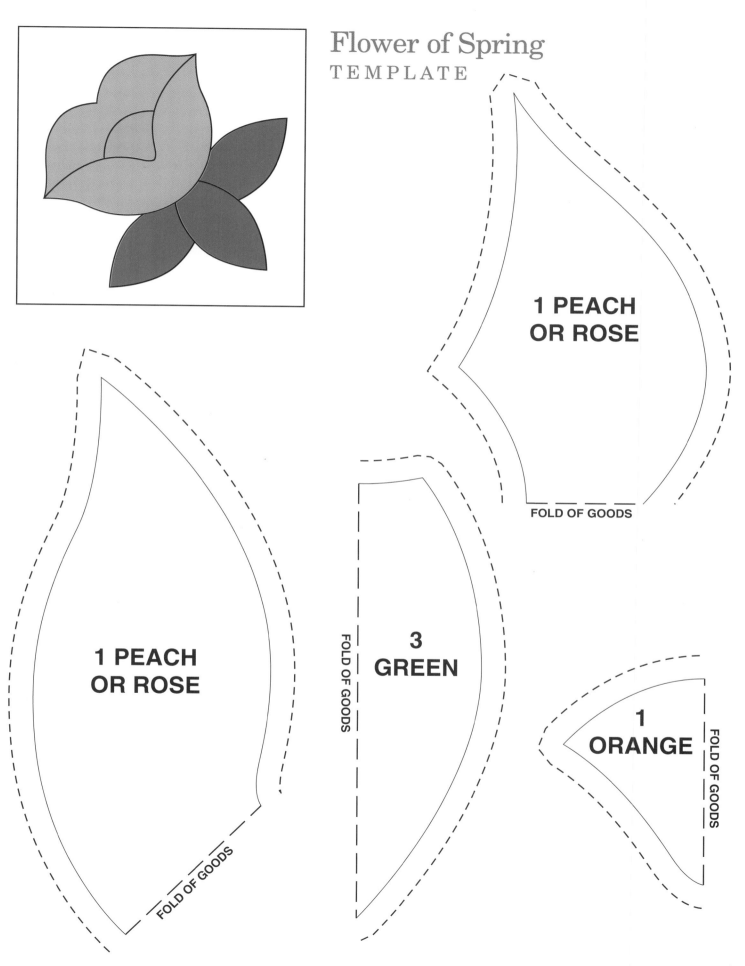

Flower of Spring
TEMPLATE

**1 PEACH
OR ROSE**

FOLD OF GOODS

**1 PEACH
OR ROSE**

FOLD OF GOODS

**3
GREEN**

FOLD OF GOODS

**1
ORANGE**

FOLD OF GOODS

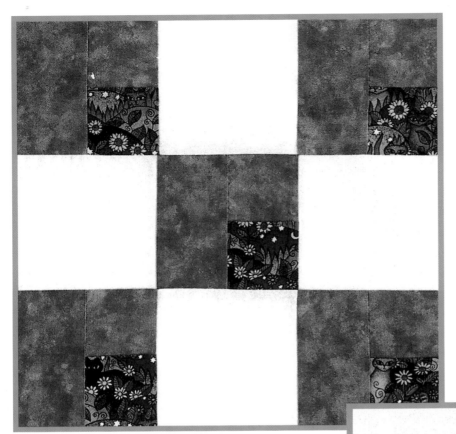

Puss in the Corner blocks made by Debbie Pulley of Peoria, Ill.

Puss IN THE Corner

I have cats. Three of them to be precise. They are called Emma Lou, Sam and Earl. All are Siamese except for Sam, he's a Himalayan. They are all characters and provide a lot of laughs and a lot of company around this house.

The first Siamese cat I had was given to me by a dear friend of my parents when I was 8-years old. Ann gave me a cat named Su Lin. Her old cat, Chafa, was up in years and Su Lin was making her last years miserable by picking on her and biting her. My mom and dad and Stormy and I had gone up to visit Ann in Silvis, Ill., in a '49 MG. Stormy and I rode in the boot behind the seats. The trip was a bit cramped on the way up and we complained about it, but that didn't hold a candle to the sheer chaos of the trip home.

My mom drove like a maniac as a matter of course. She always had one foot on the brake and one foot on the gas pedal. Whiplash was a common malady in our family, but I digress. When it came time to leave and bring the cat home, we piled into that MG. The cat was terrified. I don't know if it was travel in general

Continued on page 85.

Puss in the Corner Applique

**Original Design
By Edie McGinnis
12" Block**

Fabric needed: Dark, medium and white.

Black embroidery floss.

From dark fabric, cut one rectangle 12-1/2" x 5-1/2".

From white fabric, cut one rectangle 12-1/2" x 7-1/2".

From medium fabric, cut out the cat after tracing the pattern onto freezer paper. Be sure to add a small seam allowance when cutting.

Sew the rectangles together. Position the cat over the seam line and applique. Embroider the cat's features and collar to complete the block.

NOTE: *The seams in the rectangle may be going horizontally or vertically. If the lines are going vertically and the cat is sewn directly over the seam line, the cat appears to sit in a corner. If the seams are going in a horizontal direction, make sure the cat is appliqued into one corner of the block.*

From page 84.

that it feared or my mom's driving or the circumstances. The nice cat we put in the car became a holy terror clawing everyone in the car and howling as only a Siamese can howl.

Everyone was so grateful to get home that day. The cat was so traumatized by the two-hour trip that it hid in any corner it could find for weeks. She finally came out of her shell and slept in the crook of my knees every night and lived to the ripe old age of 19.

Puss in the Corner Applique
TEMPLATE

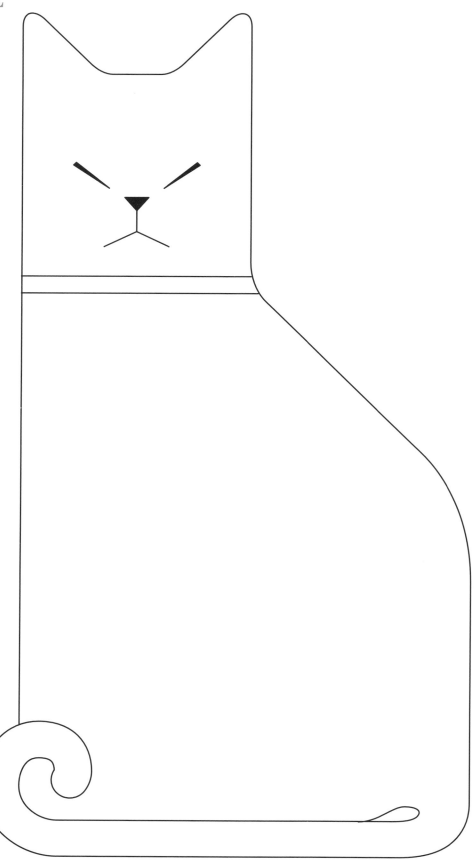

Puss in the Corner

November 5, 1932
12" Block

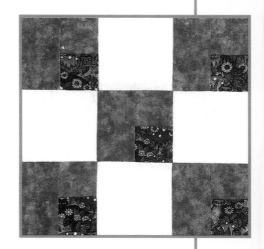

Fabric needed: dark, medium and white.

From white fabric, cut 4 4-1/2" squares.

From medium fabric, cut 5 rectangles 4-1/2" x 2-1/2" and one strip 2-1/2" x 13."

From dark fabric, cut 1 strip 2-1/2" x 13".

Sew the medium 2-1/2" strip to the dark 2-1/2" strip. With your rotary cutter, cut the strip into 2-1/2" lengths. (You will have a little extra for straightening purposes.)

Sew these units to the white squares. Your block will look like this.

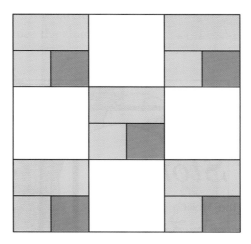

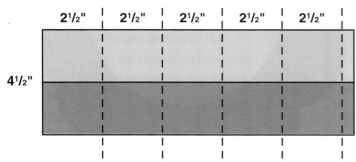

Sew the two-toned piece to the medium rectangle as shown.

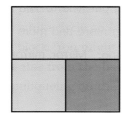

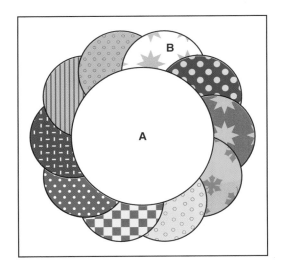

Rolling Stone Applique
TEMPLATE

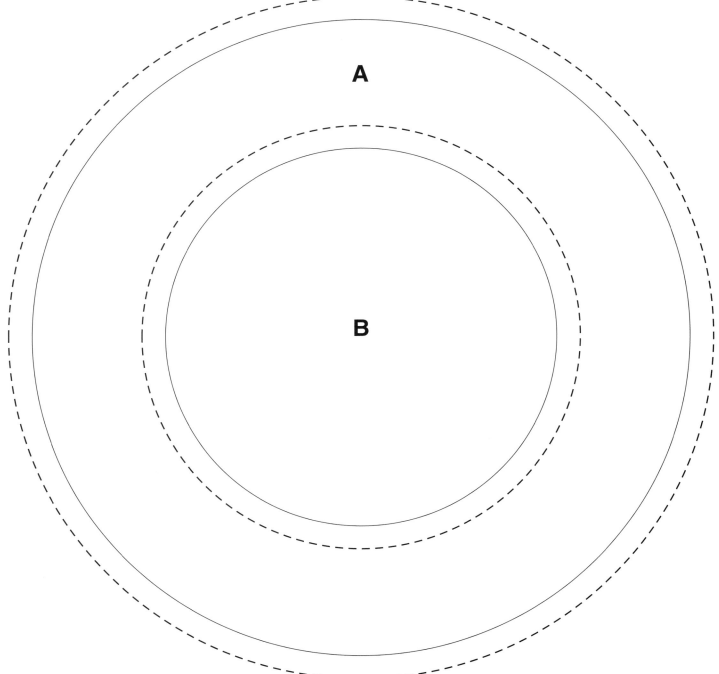

A

B

Rolling Stone

November 14, 1936
12" Block

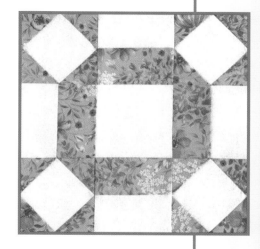

Fabric needed: white and print.

From white fabric, cut 4 squares using template A, 1 square using template C and 1 strip 2-1/2" x 19".

From the print fabric, cut 16 triangles using template B and 1 strip 2-1/2" x 19".

Sew 4 B triangles to each white A square making corner units that look like this.

Sew the white strip to the print strip and cut in 4-1/2" increments. You should have 4 of these pieces. **NOTE**: *you will have a little extra for straightening purposes.*

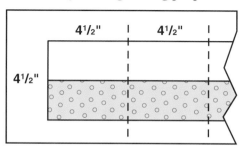

Sew a corner unit to each end of a strip unit. Make 2 of these units and set aside.

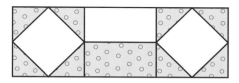

Sew the two remaining strip pieces to each side of the white square as shown.

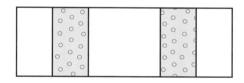

Sew the three strips together as shown to complete the block. As you can see, the white strips always face the outside of the block.

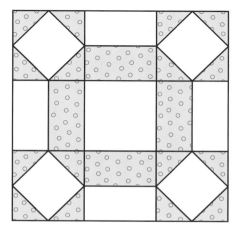

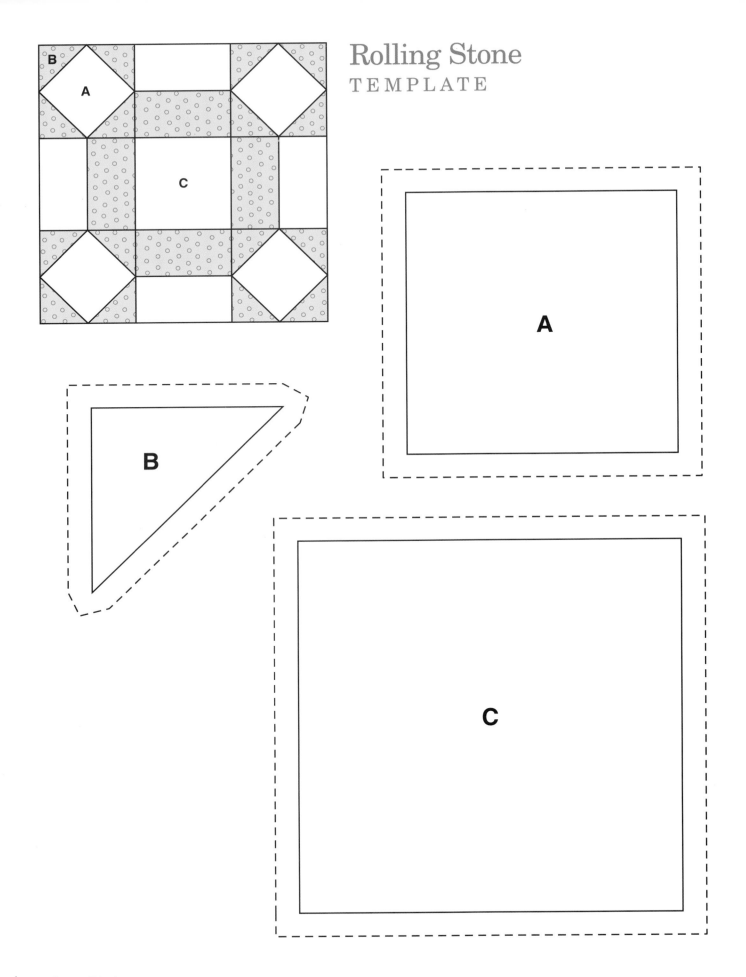

Rolling Stone
TEMPLATE

B

A

C

B

A

C

Dogwood Blossom pieced by Vera Doutt of Independence, Mo.

Dogwood Blossom block appliqued by Millie Hohimer of Independence, Mo.

THE *Dogwood Blossoms*

For the past two years I have gone to the American Quilter's Society's quilt show in Paducah, Ky. The show is held in April, a time when the dogwood trees and azaleas are blooming.

Paducah knows how to do things rights. The entire town gets behind this show. The store windows are decorated with quilts, the residents volunteer and the churches put on suppers for the quilters who come to learn, look and SHOP!

After a day at the show, a weary quilter can relax by getting into her car and driving the Dogwood Trail. The Trail is especially beautiful at night. The people of Paducah have spotlights shining on the dogwood trees and azalea bushes. The colors are lovely pink, white and red peppermint candy for the eyes.

Dogwood Applique

**Original Design
By Edie McGinnis
12" Block**

Fabric needed: pale pink, white
and green.

Brown, yellow and light green embroidery floss.

From the white fabric, cut a 12-1/2"
square. Fold the fabric into fourths
and press in the creases for placement
purposes.

Trace the pattern onto the white square.

Trace the pattern onto freezer paper.
Pin the pieces on the appropriate fabric.
Cut out the pieces, leaving a small
seam allowance.

Pin the pattern pieces into place and
applique. Embroider the brown stems
and make yellow French knots in the
center of each flower. Embroider the
lines in the leaves in light green floss to
complete the block.

Dogwood Applique
TEMPLATE

A Dogwood Blossom

September 17, 1958
12" Block

Fabric needed: dark, medium and white.

Cut 4 white and 4 dark pieces using template A.

Cut 4 white and 4 dark pieces using template B.

Cut 8 medium pieces using template C.

Cut 1 2" x 34" strip of white and one 2" x 34" strip of dark fabric. Sew the two strips together.

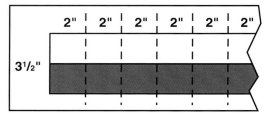

Cut the strip into 16 2" wide pieces. (You will have extra length for straightening purposes.)

Sew the strips you have just cut together to make 4-patch units as shown.

These are the corner units.

Sew a white A piece to a dark B piece. Then add a medium C piece making a unit like this.

Make a total of four of these units

Now sew a dark A piece to a white B piece. Add a medium C piece to finish the unit. It will look like this.

Make a total of 4 of these units.

Sew all the units together as shown to complete your block.

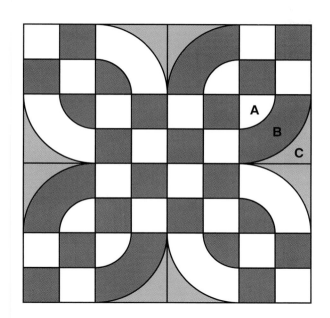

A Dogwood Blossom
TEMPLATE

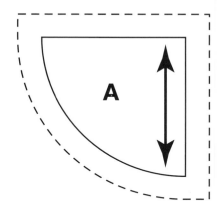

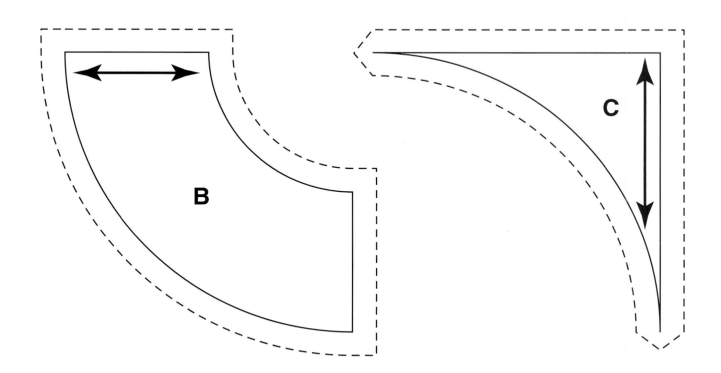

A Rosebud pieced by Alta Short of Independence, Mo.

Rose Cross appliqued by Judy Lovell of Independence, Mo.

THE
Roses

We lived on the edge of town in Tremont. I really do mean the edge of town. There were fields that Mr. Gifforn farmed on two sides of our property. Between our house and the fields was a fence row. Wild roses climbed up on the fence decorating, and hiding ugly rusted wire.

There was tall grass that grew next to the roses. I used to grab a package of saltine crackers and a good book and head for the fence row when I wanted to escape from my sisters and work. I would hide back there among the roses and pretend not to hear anyone calling for me.

The Rosebud

May 20, 1942
12" Block

Fabric needed: white, green, light red and dark red.

From the white fabric, cut 1 6-1/2" square and 4 rectangles 3-1/2" x 2" and 4 rectangles 6-1/2" x 2".

From the green fabric, cut 8 2" squares.

From the light red fabric, cut 3 10" strips.

From the dark red fabric, cut 1 10" strip.

Sew two of the light red strips together. Then sew the remaining light red strip to the dark red strip. Cut each strip into 2" increments as shown. (There will be some left over just in case you need to straighten the strips.)

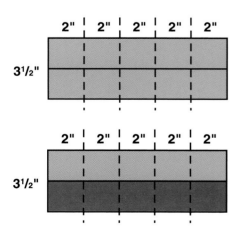

Sew the pieces you have just made together to create a 4-patch unit as shown. You should have four 4-patch units. Set these aside for the moment.

Sew a green square to each end of the 3-1/2" rectangle. Make 4 of these sections as shown below.

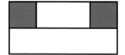

Sew a 6-1/2" white rectangle to each of the green and white rectangles as shown.

Who Made This Block

Alta Short (left) and her friend Gaynor Sandercock have become sisters through their love of quilting. Gaynor lives on a farm in the English Midlands and Alta lives in Independence, Mo. They travel back and forth to visit each other.

For the top and bottom row of the block, sew a 4-patch unit to each end of a rectangle unit. You should have two strips that look like this.

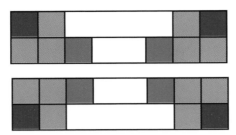

For the center row, sew a rectangle unit to each side of the large white square as shown.

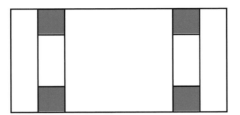

Sew the three rows together to complete the block.

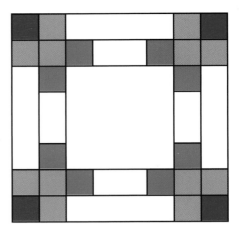

Rose Cross Applique

January 18, 1930
12" Block

Fabric needed: pink, rose, yellow, green and white.

Cut 1 12-1/2" square from the white fabric.

Cut a strip of green bias for the stems. Turn under 1/4" on each side for seam allowance.

Fold the square from corner to corner and press lightly. Refold the square from corner to corner and press lightly again. You should now have an X pressed into your fabric. This will serve as placement lines for the stems and buds and the large flower in the center.

Trace the pattern onto freezer paper and pin on the appropriate fabric. Cut out the pieces adding a small seam allowance.

Position and pin the pieces in place and applique to complete the block.

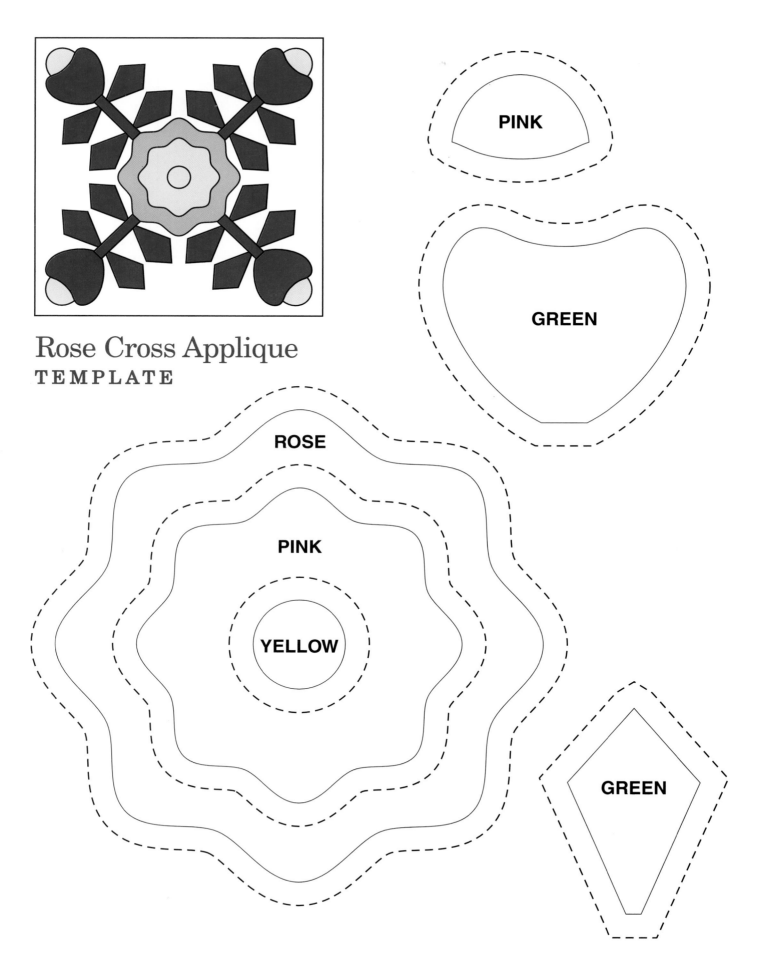

Rose Cross Applique
TEMPLATE

PINK

GREEN

ROSE

PINK

YELLOW

GREEN

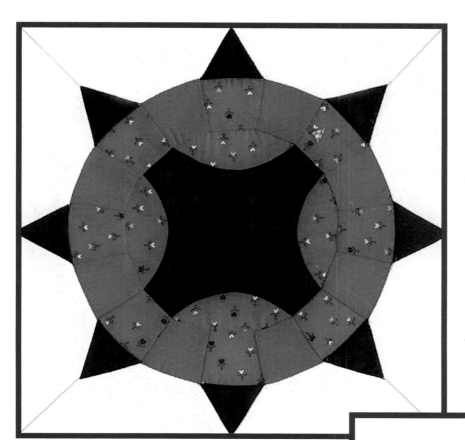

Strawberry block pieced by Helen Johnson of Independence, Mo.

Strawberry block appliqued by Nancy Dietz of Lenexa, Kan.

THE *Strawberry Blocks*

We had a strawberry patch and so did my grandma. It was our job to pick the berries in our patch and hers. I have never figured that out. I don't know why in the world anyone who expected to actually have fruit brought into the house would send us out to pick them. I guess we must have gotten some of them there because I remember my grandma making jam and my mom making strawberry shortcake.

My grandma made the kind of jam you had to boil and can. She always had a little saucer on the stove by the kettle to test the consistency. As soon as the sample had cooled, my sisters and I were waiting with a piece of bread like three little vultures. When she got tired of us being underfoot, she would send us out to the picnic table for a party with a pot of jam, some bread and tea.

The Strawberry Block

December 7, 1929
12" Block

Fabric needed: white, green, solid red and red print.

Using template A, cut 1 green piece.

Using template B, cut 4 red print ovals.

Using template C, cut 8 green pieces.

Using template D, cut 8 solid red pieces and 8 red print pieces.

Using template E, cut 4 white pieces. Reverse your template (turn it over) and cut 4 more white pieces.

Sew the 4 red print ovals to the A green piece.

Then sew a C green piece to a D red print making a unit that looks like this.

Make 8 of these units.

Make a strip by sewing a red piece to one of the C-D units you have just made. Continue sewing these together until you have used them all. Sew the strip you have just made to the circular center and close up the last seam.
Your block should look like this.

Now add the white E and E reversed pieces to complete the block.

The Strawberry Block
TEMPLATE

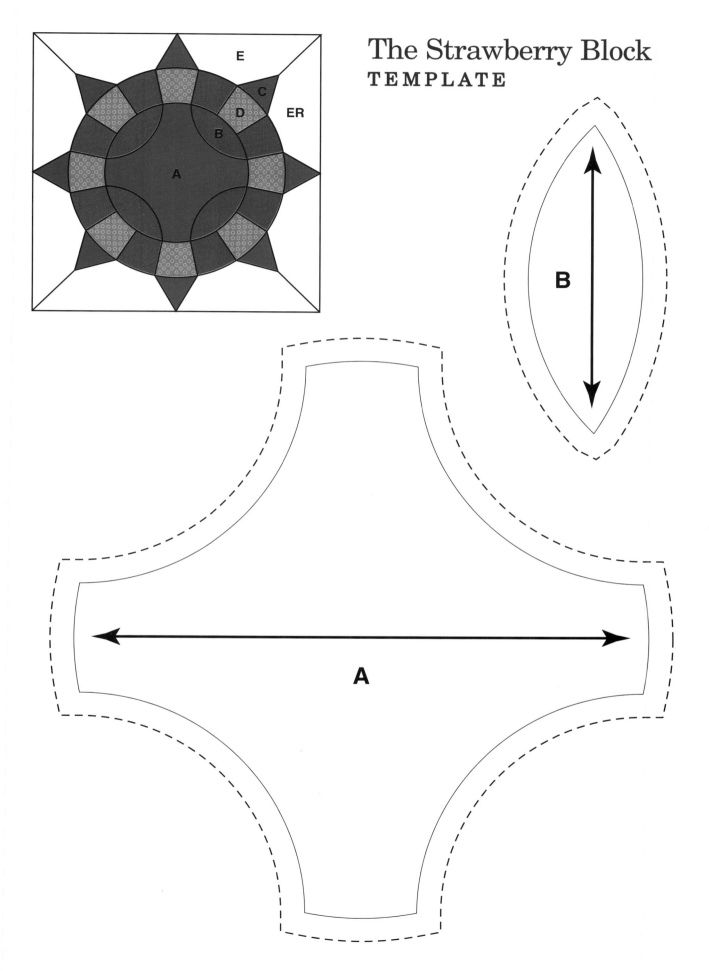

E

C

D

ER

B

A

B

A

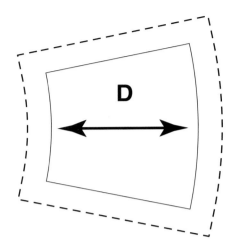

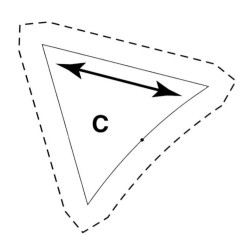

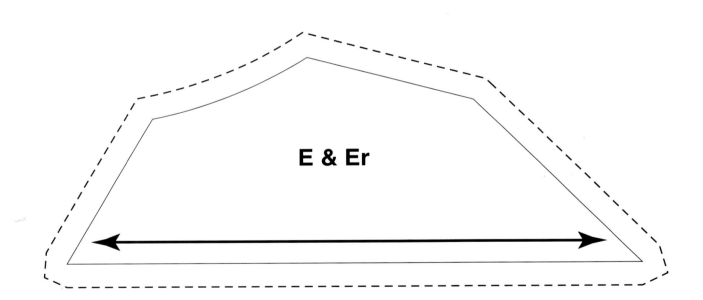

The Strawberry

Original Design
By Edie McGinnis
12" Block

Fabric needed: white, red with pin dots and tan.

Green embroidery floss.

Cut a 12-1/2" white square. Fold the square in fourths and press in the creases for placement purposes. Trace the pattern onto the white square.

Trace the pieces onto freezer paper and cut out the appropriate fabrics, adding a small seam allowance. For the handle of the basket, cut and fold a bias strip to 3/8" width.

Pin the pieces in place and applique. Position the top of the basket and applique this piece last.

Embroider the stems of the strawberries in green thread.

The basket weave marks shown are simply quilting lines to give the basket texture.

Who Made This Block

On the left is Nancy Hoffman Dietz with her sister Martha Hoffman Carnes. When this picture was taken 55 years ago, who would have thought that their mother's love of fabric arts would be such a strong influence in her daughters' lives. Nancy's older sister weaves, spins and sews and Nancy is a quilter in Lenexa, Kan.

The Strawberry
TEMPLATE

May Basket in Floral Tones block pieced by Ruby Downing of Oak Grove, Mo.

May Basket for Applique block appliqued by Betty Stubler of Smithville, Mo.

THE *May Baskets*

I remember making May Baskets as a child. My sisters and I would get out the construction paper and make flour and water paste (no sense in buying that stuff when this would work, you know). I seem to remember how the baskets all looked alike. They were cone-shaped and had a loop of paper for the handle.

While the paste was drying, we would go outside and forage for flowers to fill the baskets. About that time of the year, the lilacs and daffodils and bridal wreath were all blooming. We would pick armloads of the lilacs. They were plentiful and I think we got carried away by the fragrance.

We would go back into the house carrying our plunder. (I say that because sometimes the flowers were taken from my Grandma's yard without her permission.) We would then arrange our flowers in our baskets and go out to deliver them.

My Grandma's house was always the first target. We would hang the basket on the doorknob, knock loudly and run and hide. Our hiding place would be where we could see her open the door and find the basket of flowers. We would sit in the bushes and giggle when she would loudly wonder where in the world that May Basket had come from.

A May Basket in Floral Tones

September 17, 1947
12" Block

Who Made This Block

From left to right are Ruby Downing and sisters Eleanor Florence and Cleone Cap. This picture of the Thomas girls was taken about 1935. These three sisters have 14 quilters among their descendants who exchange fabric and have "show and tell" at their annual family reunions.

Fabric needed: white and floral tones.

AUTHOR'S NOTE: *Ordinarily I wouldn't give templates for this pattern but since the grid is a 5 patch on a 12" block, the measurements are a little odd so I am recommending the use of templates.*

From white fabric, cut 1 square using template A, three large triangles using template E, two triangles using template C, 4 triangles using template B and 2 rectangles using template D.

From the floral toned fabric, cut 12 triangles using template B and 1 triangle using template E.

Sew a colored E triangle to a white E triangle making a square as shown.

Sew 3 B triangles together. Start with a colored triangle, then add a white triangle and end with a colored triangle as shown.

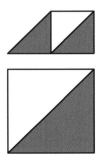

Sew these to the top of the square.

Sew three more B triangles together as shown and sew them to the left side of the square. Your block should look like this.

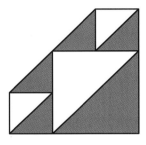

Now add a white E triangle. You now have a square that looks like this.

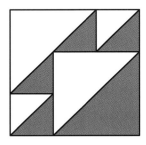

Sew two B triangles together using a white and a color. Sew two colored B triangles to a C white triangle as shown.

Sew these two units together and attach them to the left side of the square as shown.

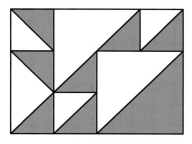

For the top row, sew 2 B triangles together making a square.

Sew 2 B triangles to 2 sides of a C triangle as shown.

Beginning with the white A square, add the two units you just made like this.

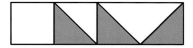

Sew the strip to the top of the block. Your block should look like this.

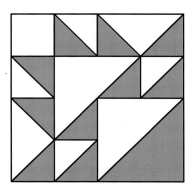

Now sew a B triangle to each white D rectangle and add these to the block as shown.

Add the remaining white E triangle to the corner to complete the block.

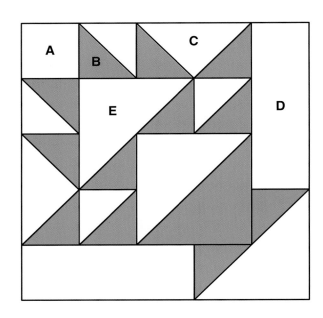

A May Basket
in Floral Tones
TEMPLATE

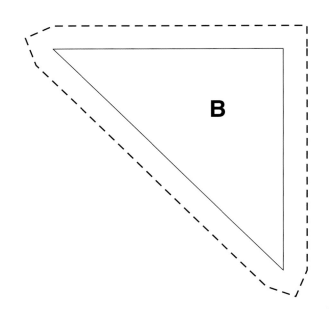

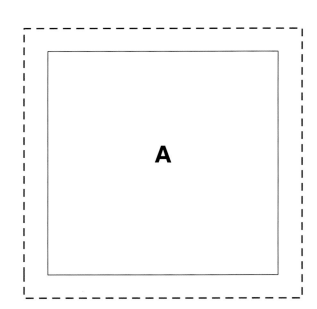

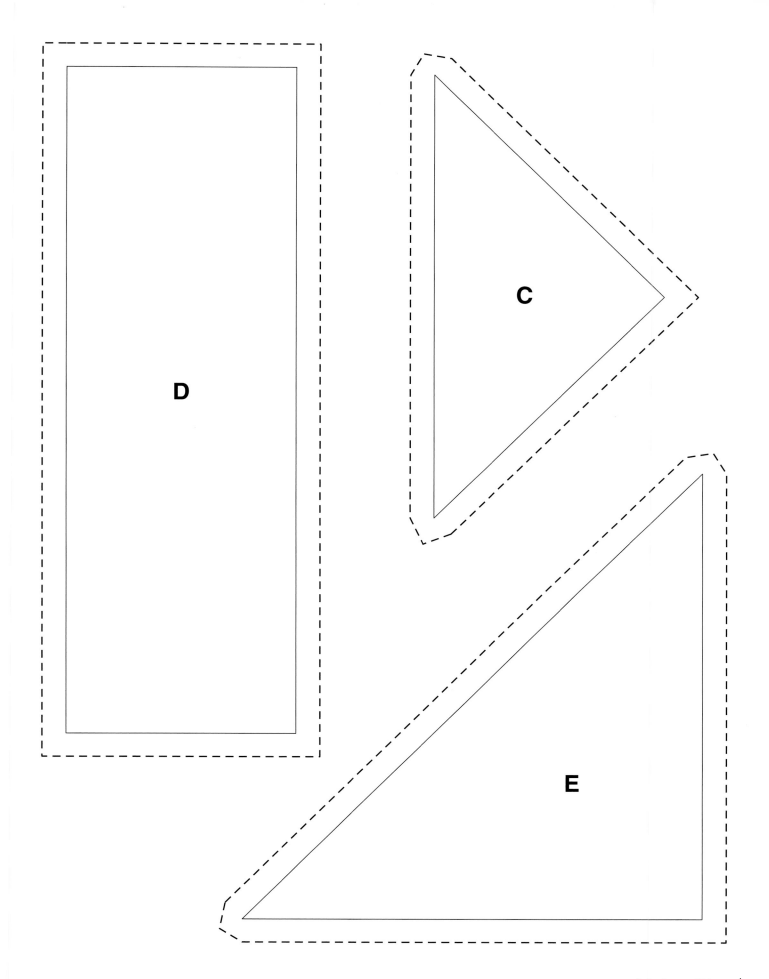

D

C

E

May Basket for Applique

August 28, 1946
12" Block

Fabric needed: green, dark green, pink, yellow, blue and white.

From the white, cut 1 12-1/2" square. Fold the square in quarters and press in the creases for placement purposes.

Trace the basket design onto the white square.

Trace the pieces onto freezer paper and cut them out of the appropriate colors, adding a small seam allowance. Pin the pieces in place and applique to complete the block.

NOTE: *Since the original pattern does not specify what color to use for the basket other than the green strips, you might want to use the same yellow that was used for the flower centers.*

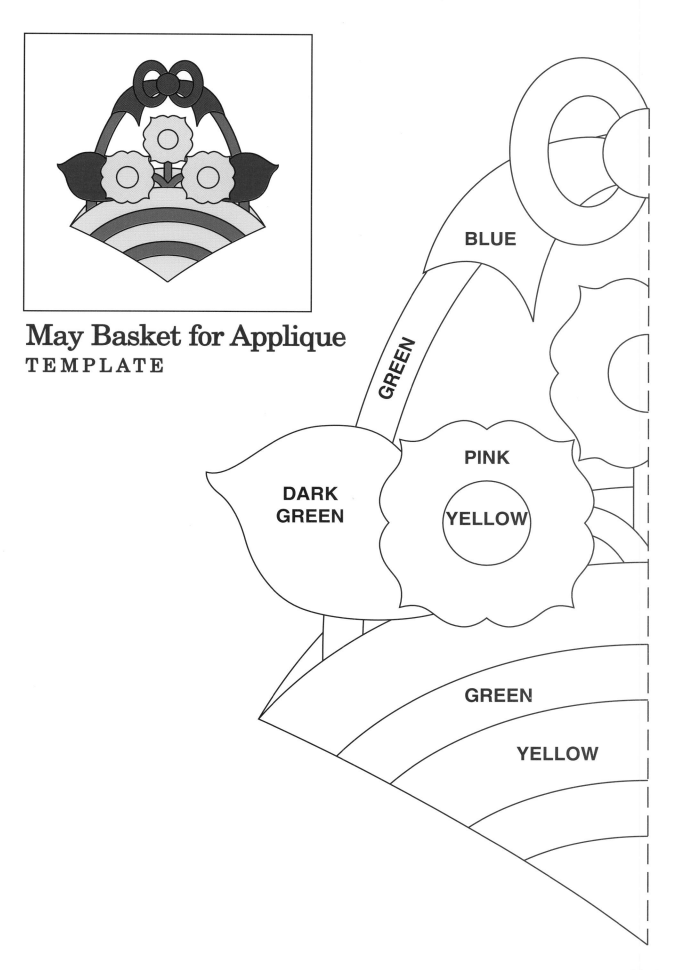

May Basket for Applique
TEMPLATE

BLUE

GREEN

DARK GREEN

PINK

YELLOW

GREEN

YELLOW

Four Leaf Clover and Shamrock blocks made by Clara Diaz of Independence, Mo.

Shamrock AND Four Leaf Clover

My mother passed away three years ago. It was left to me to go through everything because she lived close to me. She had a great many books and in some of them she had pressed flowers between the pages. She was very fond of four-leaf clovers and must have saved every one she found.

When I opened the pages of some of the old books, little crumbles of the edges of the flowers would sift out. Sometimes I would get lost in the memories of my mom and my sisters and me sitting in the yard on a hot summer day. We would run our hands through the patches of clover searching for some good luck. My mom always found the four-leaf clovers. When we got bored with that we would make bracelets and wreaths out of the clover blossoms.

Shamrock

March 19, 1932
12" Block

Fabric needed: White and green.

Green embroidery floss.

From the white fabric, cut 1 12-1/2"
square. Fold the square in fourths and
press lightly. The creases are used for
placement purposes.

Trace the heart on freezer paper and cut
out 12 green hearts, adding a seam
allowance. Pin the hearts on the white
square and applique in place. Embroider
the stems to complete the block.

Who Made This Block

Clara Diaz is shown with
three of her sisters. In the
front are (from left) Ann
Hetrick and Paula Richards
and in the back are Marie
Rogers and Clara Diaz. Marie
and Clara were wearing
matching skirts made from
feedsack fabric by their grandmother.

Shamrock
TEMPLATE

12 GREEN

Four Leaf Clover

September 25, 1935
12" Block

Fabric needed: white, green and red.

From green fabric, cut 4 ovals using template A and 8 half-ovals using template E.

From red fabric, cut 16 pieces using template B and 4 squares using template C.

From white fabric, cut 16 pieces using template D.

Sew a red B piece to either side of a white D piece.

Sew a white D piece to each side of a red square, making sure the curve of the D pieces always face to the outside of the block.

Sew a red B piece to either side of a white D piece.

You now have three strips. Sew them together to make a nine-patch unit. Make 3 more of these units.

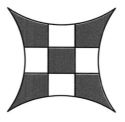

Sew a unit to each side of a green oval. Do this twice so you have two segments that look like this.

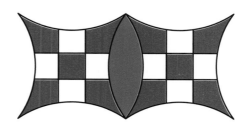

Sew two green ovals onto the bottom of one of the segments.

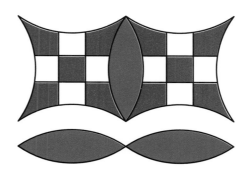

Add the other nine-patch segment to the curves.

Your block will look like this.

Add the green half-ovals all the way around to complete the block.

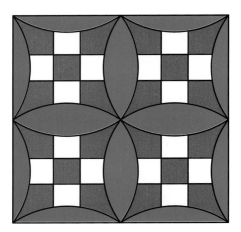

NOTE: *If you want to make a quilt like this, use full ovals to connect the blocks together. Only use the half ovals on the outside of the blocks to square the quilt.*

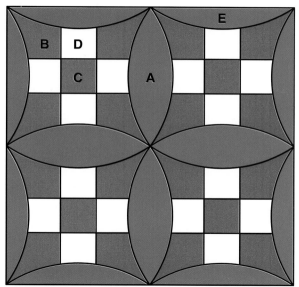

Four Leaf Clover
TEMPLATE

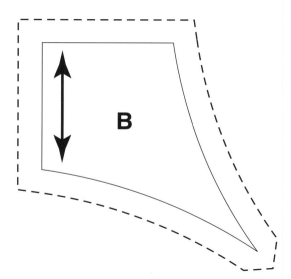

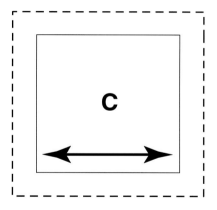

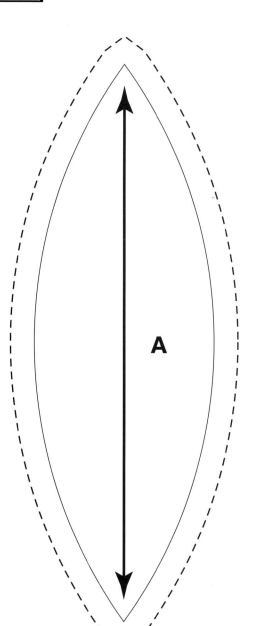

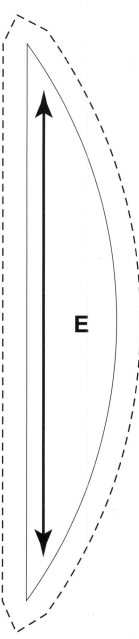

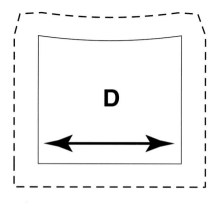

With more than 1,000 patterns, the Kansas City Stars offer projects for everyone from novices to advanced quilters.

If you're a beginner but would like to try making an entire quilt, here are basic, complete directions for a full-size (72-by-96-inch) Double Square. Quilting books with more detailed instructions are available at quilt shops or your public library.

Terms in boldface are defined in the accompanying glossary.

Cutting

Machine-wash each fabric separately, using the detergent and temperature settings you plan to use to clean it after it becomes a quilt. Check for shrinkage and color fastness. With most modern fabrics, neither of these is a problem, but occasionally fabrics can shrink and colors can run. You don't want to find this out after your quilt is finished. If all is well, press each fabric and trim off selvages using your rotary cutter and rotary ruler.

Make sure all fabric edges are straight. Do this by folding the fabric in half lengthwise and aligning the long edges with horizontal lines on a rotary cutting mat. If edges along the width aren't straight, align your rotary-cutting ruler with a vertical line and cut straight across the width as

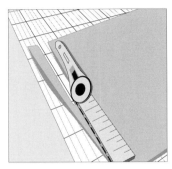

Diagram 1

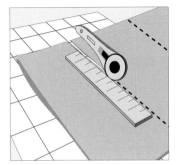

Diagram 2

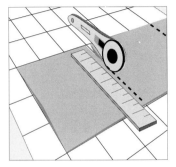

Diagram 3

Materials

These are available at quilt or craft stores. Words in **boldface** are defined in the glossary at the end of this chapter.

4½ yards of dark fabric, 100 percent cotton
3½ yards of light fabric, 100 percent cotton
7½ yards of fabric for **backing**, 100 percent cotton
Double/queen size **batting** (cotton or polyfill)
Template plastic with grids
Rotary cutter

Rotary mat
Pins
Quilting thread
Quilting needles (betweens)
Quilting thimble
Wash-out marking pencils
24-by-6-inch clear ruler with grids
Quilting hoop

close to the edge as possible to save fabric (Diagram 1).

Now move the ruler 6C\v inches in from the edge and cut across the width of the fabric (Diagram 2). Repeat until you have 16 strips of dark fabric and 16 of light. Set aside remaining dark material for later use. Line up strips and cut into 6C\v-inch squares (Diagram 3).

Cut these squares from corner to corner at a 45-degree angle (Diagram 4). You will have 192 dark triangles and 192 light triangles.

Piecing

You can **piece** your quilt by hand or machine. There are advantages to each.

With hand piecing, you don't need a sewing machine. Your project is portable. You can hand-piece just about anywhere, and many quilters enjoy taking their projects along with them.

Machine piecing, however, is a lot faster.

For this quilt, if you're piecing by hand: Place your template plastic over the template pattern for the Double Square (See page 143). Trace on dashed lines.

Cut out template with scissors.

Place the template on the **wrong side** of the fabric. Trace around the template with marking pencil on each triangular piece of fabric. These are sewing lines.

If you're piecing by machine, marking your sewing lines isn't necessary. Use the ¼-inch **seam guide** on your machine.

With the **right sides** of the fabric facing each other, place together the long sides of 1 light triangle and 1 dark triangle. Match the corners along the long side and pin on the seam line. With a small **running stitch**, sew along the marked seam line. Unfold and you'll have a square that is half dark and half light (Diagram 5).

Repeat on 3 more sets of triangles for a total of 4 squares.

Sew 2 squares together, placing dark triangle against light as shown in Diagram 6. Sew 2 more squares together the same way.

Place those 2 rectangles together and sew as shown in Diagram 7. This makes 1 complete block.

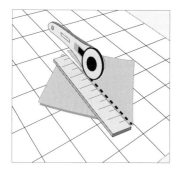

Diagram 4

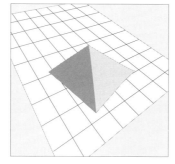

Diagram 5

Diagram 6

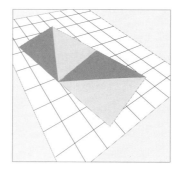

Diagram 7

Diagram 8

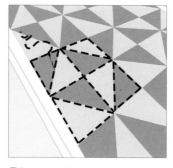

Diagram 9

Repeat the process until 48 blocks are complete.

Sew 6 blocks together into strip. Make 8 strips. Sew strips together to complete the **quilt top** (Diagram 8). Before you sew together each block and each strip, pin each part together, taking care to keep all corners and intersecting seams matched.

Backing

Fold the backing fabric in half lengthwise. Cut across the width into two parts, each 3¾ yards long. Place the parts together, right sides facing each other. Sew pieces together along the length of fabric. This forms the back of the quilt.

Assembly

Iron the quilt top with all **seams** going toward the dark piece. On the back, press the middle seam open. This makes it easier to quilt through the seam.

Place backing, right side *down*, on a flat surface; smooth out all wrinkles. Place the quilt **batting** atop the backing. Place the top on these, right side *up*. **Baste** all layers together with thread or safety pins 4 to 6 inches apart in a rough grid. If you baste with thread, remove the stitches only after finishing the quilting. If you use safety pins, remove them as you quilt.

Quilting

You are now ready to begin **quilting**.

Place your quilting hoop as near the center as possible. You'll work from the center out toward the edges, moving the hoop as you complete each area.

Thread your quilting needle and put a small knot at one end of the thread. Thread directly from the spool to minimize tangles.

Mark the quilting line on each block ¼ inch in from each seam line with fine-line, wash-out marking pencil or with ¼-inch quilter's masking tape.

To start the first stitch, slide the needle in anywhere under the first layer and pull the needle up to a marked quilting line. Tug gently until the knot pulls through the starting point and catches between the layers. That way, the knot will be hidden

Continue quilting as shown in Diagram 9. Try to make stitches as small and even as possible.

When you're almost out of thread, tie a knot in the thread closest to the quilt top. Insert your needle through the top layer, through the batting and back out the top, lodging the knot in the batting. Cut the remaining thread,

rethread the needle and repeat the process.

Binding

After all quilting is complete, you'll need to **bind** the quilt.

Trim all excess batting and backing from the edges. Using the dark fabric set aside earlier, cut 10 strips horizontally, each 2½ inches wide.

Sew the ends of 2 strips together across their width. The resulting strip will be long enough to go across the top edge of the quilt. Sew 2 more strips together in the same manner to go across the bottom edge of the quilt. Now sew

Diagram 10

3 strips together to go on each side of the quilt. Fold each strip in half length-

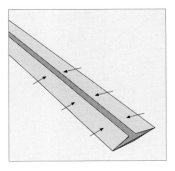

Diagram 11

Diagram 12

wise and press (Diagram 10). Then fold one side of

each strip halfway in and press. Bring the other side

over until edges meet and press again (Diagram 11).

Sew the strip to the top of quilt with a running stitch (Diagram 12). Turn the remaining binding to the back and stitch. Do the side edges of the quilt first. Then do the top and bottom edges, folding under the raw ends of the binding to make the corners neat.

Your *Kansas City Star* quilt is complete!

QUILT GLOSSARY

■ **Background (or secondary) fabric:** A secondary fabric that complements the predominant fabric used in a quilt. (See also *primary fabric*.)

■ **Backing:** The bottom layer of a quilt.

■ **Baste:** Pinning or loosely stitching layers of a quilt together in preparation for quilting. The pins or stitches are later removed and the quilting holds all the layers of the quilt together.

■ **Batting:** The middle layer of the quilt, which provides depth and warmth. Batting, mainly cotton or polyester, is sold in lofts; a high loft is thick, a low loft is thin. The thinner the loft, the easier it is to quilt.

■ **Binding:** A strip of fabric used to enclose the rough edges of all the layers of a finished quilt.

■ **Block:** A square unit consisting of pieces of fabric sewn into a design. Many blocks sewn together make a quilt top.

■ **4-patch:** A square block using four pieces of fabric.

■ **9-patch:** A square block using nine pieces of fabric.

■ **Piecing:** Stitching together quilt pieces.

■ **Press to, press away:** To iron the fabric in a block. "Press to dark" means iron both sides of the seam toward the darker fabric; "press to the edge" means iron both sides of the seam toward the outer edge of the fabric, and so on. "Press away" means the opposite, as in "press away from center."

■ **Primary fabric:** The predominant fabric used in a quilt.

■ **Quilting:** Stitching through the top, middle and bottom layers of a quilt in a design or in straight lines to secure the layers together and add a decorative touch.

■ **Quilting hoop:** A two-part wooden or plastic circle. Placed on either side of the quilt, the hoop holds the fabric taut inside.

■ **Quilting needles:** Smaller than sewing needles, quilting needles are called "betweens." They come in sizes from 7 (longest) to 12 (shortest). Beginning quilters often use a 7 or 8.

■ **Quilting thimble:** A thimble with a ridge around the top to help push the quilting needle.

■ **Quilting thread:** Heavier and stronger than average sewing thread.

■ **Right side:** The front side of the fabric with a pattern or color; the opposite of the "wrong side," or back of a fabric.

■ **Rotary cutter:** A sharp, circular cutting utensil — resembling a pizza cutter — used to cut through layers of fabric.

■ **Rotary mat:** A mat marked with grids and angles, made to be used with a rotary cutter.

■ **Running stitch:** A sewing stitch made by passing the needle in and out repeatedly, using short, even stitches.

■ **Selvages:** The lengthwise, finished edges of a fabric.

■ **Seams:** The line formed by sewing together pieces of fabric.

■ **Seam guide:** A mark or piece on a sewing machine footplate that measures the distance from the needle to the edge of the fabric.

■ **Template:** A pattern, usually plastic, used to trace cutting or sewing lines onto fabric.

■ **Wrong side:** See **Right side.**

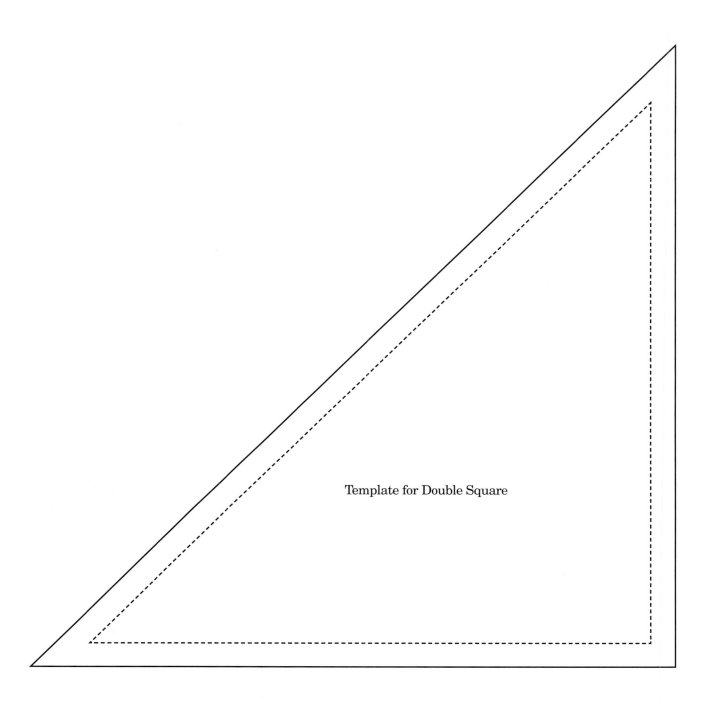

Template for Double Square

THE QUILTS, YEAR BY YEAR

Here is a chronological list — including repeats — of the quilt patterns and designs published by *The Kansas City Star* from 1928 through the present.

If you'd like to see the patterns on the pages of the newspaper, microfilm copies of *The Star* are available at the Kansas City Public Library's Main Branch, 311 E. 12th St., Kansas City, Mo.

For an alphabetical list of the designs, see Wilene Smith's *Quilt Patterns: An Index to The Kansas City Star Patterns* (details in Bibliography).

For a thumbnail sketch of each pattern, see Volume 5 of *The Ultimate Illustrated Index to The Kansas City Star Quilt Pattern Collection* by the Central Oklahoma Quilters Guild (details in Bibliography).

Months not listed here had no published quilt patterns.

1928

■ **September**
Pine Tree
Album Quilt
■ **October**
French Star
Log Cabin
Rob Peter and Pay Paul
Cherry Basket
Wedding Ring
■ **November**
Jacob's Ladder
Greek Cross
Sky Rocket
Double T
■ **December**
Ocean Wave
Wild Goose Chase
Old Maid's Puzzle
Rambler

1929

■ **January**
Weathervane
Monkey Wrench
Spider Web
Irish Chain
■ **February**
Rising Sun
Princess Feather
Double Nine Patch
Eight-Pointed Star
■ **March**
Goose in the Pond
Dove in the Window
Beautiful Star
Broken Circle
Beggar Block
■ **April**
Cupid's Arrow Point
Noon Day Lily
Lafayette Orange Peel
Necktie
■ **May**
Duck and Ducklings
House on the Hill
Crossed Canoes
Turkey Tracks
■ **June**
Ribbon Border Block
Posey
Bird's Nest

Crosses and Losses
Double Star
■ **July**
Jack in the Box
Aircraft
Springtime Blossoms
Sunbeam
■ **August**
Saw-Tooth
Cross and Crown
Hands All 'Round
Honey Bee
Flower Pot
■ **September**
Susannah
Goose Tracks
Fish Block
Wedding Ring
■ **October**
Swastika
Seth Thomas Rose
"V" Block
Little Beech Tree
■ **November**
Palm Leaf
Tulip Applique
Mill Wheel
Order No. 11
Old King Cole's Crown
■ **December**
Strawberry Block
Old King Cole
Little Wooden Soldier
Road to Oklahoma
(The "Santa's Parade
Quilt" series ran
in December 1929).

1930

■ **January**
Churn Dash
Corn and Beans
Rose Cross
Milky Way
■ **February**
True Lovers Buggy
Wheel
Indiana Puzzle
Blazing Star
Aster
■ **March**
Sunflower
Grape Basket

Steps to the Altar
Kaleidoscope
Dutchman's Puzzle
■ **April**
English Flower Garden
Single Wedding Ring
Pin Wheels
Cross and Crown
■ **May**
Missouri Puzzle
Merry Go-Round
Lone Star
Missouri Star
Sail Boat
■ **June**
Virginia Star
Rail Fence
■ **July**
Mexican Star
Basket of Oranges
Rose Album
Clay's Choice
■ **August**
Maple Leaf
Sunbonnet Sue
Compass
Kaleidoscope
Rainbow Tile
■ **September**
Goblet
Calico Puzzle
Broken Dishes
Swallows in the Window
■ **October**
Secret Drawer
Spider Web
Marble Floor
Pinwheel
(The "Memory Bouquet
Quilt" series ran
in October 1930.)
■ **November**
Grandmother's Favorite
Indian Emblem
Friendship
Puss in the Corner
Sage-Bud
(The "Memory Bouquet
Quilt" series ran
in November 1930).
■ **December**
Turnabout "T"
Snow Crystals

Sweet Gum Leaf
Rose Dream

1931

■ **January**
Silver and Gold
Tennessee Star
Flower Pot
Greek Cross
Sheep Fold
■ **February**
Amethyst
Wheel of Mystery
Pontiac Star
Baby Bunting
■ **March**
Seven Stars
Rebecca's Fan
French Bouquet
Casement Window
■ **April**
Basket of Lilies
King's Crown
June Butterfly
Fence Row
■ **May**
Indian Trail
English Ivy
Jackson Star
Dutch Tulip
Love Ring
■ **June**
Ararat
Iris Leaf
Ozark Diamond
Kite Quilt
■ **July**
Cactus Flower
Arrowhead Star
Giddap
Sugar Loaf
■ **August**
Cross Roads
Bachelor's Puzzle
Morning Star
Pineapple Quilt
Dresden Plate
■ **September**
Stepping Stones
Tennessee Star
Chips and Whetstones
Boutonniere

■ **October**
Prickly Pear
Castle Wall
Butterfly
Pickle Dish
Dutch Tile
■ **November**
Cottage Tulips
Formosa Tea Leaf
Bridge
Evening Star
■ **December**
Poinsettia
Goldfish
Christmas Star
Crazy Daisy

1932

■ **January**
Friendship Knot
Circular Saw
Heart's Desire
Job's Tears
Necktie
(The "Horn of Plenty
Quilt" series also ran
in January 1932).
■ **February**
Autograph Quilt
Hour-Glass
Spring Beauty
Grandmother's Basket
(The "Horn of Plenty
Quilt" series also ran
in February 1932).
■ **March**
Grandmother's Favorite
Quilting Design
Shamrock
Magnolia Bud
■ **April**
Nose-Gay
Diamond Field
Red Cross
Solomon's Puzzle
"4-H" Club
■ **May**
Russian Sunflower
Storm at Sea
Crow's Nest
Garden Maze
■ **June**
Cowboy's Star

INDEX OF PATTERNS

INDEX OF PATTERNS

INDEX OF PATTERNS

INDEX OF PATTERNS